Vancouver Cooks

edited by
JAMIE MAW
and
JOAN CROSS
—

CHEFS'
TABLE
SOCIETY
*of british
columbia*

C O O K S

DOUGLAS
& McINTYRE

—

*Vancouver
Toronto*

Douglas & McIntyre
2323 Quebec Street, Suite 201
Vancouver, British Columbia
Canada v5t 4s7
www.douglas-mcintyre.com

Library and Archvies Canada Cataloguing in Publication
Vancouver cooks / the Chefs' Table Society of British Columbia ; edited by Jamie Maw and Joan Cross ; foreword by John Bishop.

Includes index.
ISBN 1-55365-028-X

1. Cookery, Canadian—British Columbia style.
2. Cookery—British Columbia—Vancouver. 3. Cookery—British Columbia. I. Maw, Jamie, 1952– II. Cross, Joan, 1939– III. Chefs' Table Society of British Columbia
TX715.6.v365 2004   641.59711'33   c2004-903242-9

The Chefs' Table Society of British Columbia is a registered non-profit society whose mission is to secure apprenticeships for and bestow bursaries to emerging local chefs. The founding directors of this society are Julian Bond, Patrick Corsi, Robert Clark, Sid Cross, Jack Evrensel, Robert Feenie, Thomas Haas, Jamie Maw, Sinclair Philip and Vikram Vij.

Cover and interior design by Peter Cocking
Cover photograph by Shannon Mendes
Editors: Jamie Maw and Joan Cross
Wine editor: Sid Cross
Associate editors: Jane Mundy and Tiffany Soper
Text editors: Lucy Kenward and Saeko Usukawa
Interior photography: John Sherlock (colour images) and Shannon Mendes (black and white images)
Food styling: Murray Bancroft
Logistics: Sue Alexander, Annabel Hawksworth, Cate Simpson, Tanis Tsisserev and Nancy Wong
Marketing and Distribution: Barbara-jo McIntosh
Printed and bound in Canada by Friesens
Printed on acid-free paper

The publisher gratefully acknowledges the financial support of the Canada Council for the Arts, the British Columbia Arts Council, and the Government of Canada through the Book Publishing Industry Development Program (BPIDP) for its publishing activities.

Contents

A WARM WELCOME to the chefs' table, to the best seat in the house. The fires are banked, the stoves hot, the *mise en place* complete, the pantry fully stocked. Fully stocked, I'll add, with some of the greatest ingredients in the world. And now our kitchen is staffed with an outstanding brigade of chefs, some astonishingly young, and their recipes, which are simply delicious.

I am thrilled to be introducing this special cookbook. It contains a wealth of recipes, and also—like a coming-of-age chronicle—recognizes the work of talented chefs from Vancouver, Vancouver Island, Whistler and the burgeoning Okanagan Valley wine country. Each day, these chefs enrich our lives, and their recipes tell the real story of how our west coast cuisine has evolved.

This cookbook captures barely contained passion on each page. It's the passion of our province's chefs, a passion born in the Pacific and filled with will and determination and pure culinary talent. Combine this talent with ingredients grown locally and picked season by season—and you have the makings of a culinary epicentre. British Columbia's cuisine is now so distinctive it tells us that we could only be eating here.

Whether you are a professional chef or an enthusiastic home cook, these are truly exciting times, because our access to fine

ingredients is unrivalled in North America. And now, with this book, comes the opportunity to replicate some of the cooking from the great chefs of our province.

For the longest time we didn't know just how rich we are in our own backyards. To write this message, I looked back (with not a little nostalgia) at menus and dining guides from the 1970s and early '80s, when I was getting my start. I was shocked to see how little focus there was in those days on fresh local ingredients. I don't think we thought of them as being special enough; we certainly would not have considered serving local seafood as part of a fine dining meal. Instead we offered the imported delicacies of the day: escargot, Dover sole, Icelandic scampi or eastern seaboard lobster. Why, even oysters were imported, and we ate them cooked—à la Mr. Rockefeller. Finally, we are embracing our own wonderful ingredients.

Vancouver is a very different place today than when I arrived thirty years ago. There were many fewer fine dining restaurants then; many were in hotels or private clubs. Now there are many options, many styles, many cuisines. We are spoiled for choice. And we are also changing the way we think about dining, choosing a less formal approach to eating out, increasingly ordering from tasting menus composed of a series of small dishes. We find fine food in relaxed surroundings. But let's not forget where this kind of dining came from: Vancouver is home to some of the best Asian cuisine and chefs anywhere, and these chefs have mightily influenced our regional cuisine, leaving a bold mark on all our cooking styles. We're very fortunate for our diversity: we have a varied and wide-ranging group of talented chefs who represent both Asian and European cuisines. You will find many of their recipes in these pages.

Throughout this book, our chefs marry their individual dialects to local ingredients. There is wild salmon from our northern rivers and ocean, Dungeness crab and giant halibut from the mystical Queen Charlotte Islands, and oysters, clams and mussels of every shape and size from the surrounding waters. Other indigenous foods such as sea lettuce, kelp and sea asparagus are harvested along the coastal shores, and fiddlehead ferns come in the early spring from Vancouver Island. There is also locally raised lamb, free-run poultry, and depending on the season, a whole slew of hand-picked wild morels and chanterelles.

Just a few hours drive from the city lie the rich, giant gardens of the Okanagan-Similkameen, Pemberton, Hazelmere and Fraser valleys. These gardens, with their own micro climates, grow a huge diversity of heirloom and organic crops—tree fruits, stone fruits, melons, tomatoes, luscious leafy greens, white asparagus, many varieties of squashes and root vegetables, potatoes, onions and garlic. Even bananas are being cultivated in the warm desert climate around Osoyoos.

And, of course, grapes are being grown throughout the Okanagan Valley, the Gulf and Vancouver Islands and elsewhere in the province. Talented winemakers are producing wines using all of the major European grape varietals, and our Rieslings, Pinot Gris and Pinot Blancs complement local seafood like no others. Intense icewines are exported around the world. And now rich reds from the southern Okanagan include Merlot, Syrah and Cabernet Sauvignon. We also have a fine selection of locally crafted artisanal cheeses with names like Blossom's Blue, Tiger Blue, White Grace, Marcella and Juliette that pair so well with these wines. Serve them with some locally handmade Oyama sausage.

We all love this place, with its beautiful mountains, river valleys, oceans and islands. Now here is a powerful way to touch the land and sea again—to connect with their bounty. Let's sit a while and savour it.

JOHN BISHOP

COLLABORATIONS achieve results that no individual could attain alone, and the Chefs' Table Society is no different. A collaboration of British Columbia's outstanding chefs and culinary professionals—each dedicated to aggressively sourcing local, seasonal, sustainable ingredients—the society meets several times a year to discuss products, challenges and the sheer joy of cooking here. Time and again, this free exchange of ideas and resources sparks new ideas and creative solutions that enrich the group as a whole.

Like many of the best ideas, this cookbook was begun over several glasses of wine and platters of great food. Not one chef, of the many in the room at Lumière that day or at the following meetings scattered around the province, questioned the idea. From the outset, a book of recipes from British Columbia's finest chefs preparing dishes made from the province's local bounty seemed natural and timely. Soon each chef was at work, preparing distinctive recipes that are reflective of where we live. Now they are yours.

We are justifiably proud of our local larder, and although restaurants continue to import outstanding products from far afield, the rediscovery of what's in our own backyards has forged a local food culture as diverse as any in the world. As our local cuisine emerges from many, you will find flavours from these recipes that reach out around the world but always return right here.

Putting together this feast was possible only because of a lengthy list of volunteers and culinary professionals. We thank them all, a remarkably dedicated and directed group. I would like to signal the special efforts of several. Logistical suppport was provided by the intrepid Annabel Hawksworth, Cate Simpson, Tanis Tsisserev and Nancy Wong. Jane Mundy ably assisted in recipe testing and provisioning. Sue Alexander and Tiffany Soper of Alexander Ink provided organizational support that moved the large cast of contributors forward gracefully. Sid Cross, whose wine mnemonics are legendary, begat the wine pairings. Murray Bancroft expertly styled the food and facilitated the photo shoots. And John Sherlock and Shannon Mendes, through their exemplary photography, brought light to these pages.

But I reserve singular thanks for Joan Cross, my co-editor. The always gracious Joan, who is a skilled and gifted cook in her own right, tested all of the recipes. It was a huge job. Joan also organized several dinner parties, at which we crafted the chefs' recipes and then evaluated them to ensure that each recipe would be enjoyable to shop for and prepare at home, and that the results would be deeply flavoursome. They are.

Proceeds from the sale of this book are deeded to the Chefs' Table Society of British Columbia, a registered non-profit society. They will secure apprenticeships and bestow bursaries to emerging local chefs.

So here we share with you the fruits of our collaboration and trust that the joy and the passion of these pages will soon reach into your very own kitchen. Enjoy.

JAMIE MAW

List of Recipes

Wild Spring Salmon en Papillote

with Fresh Peaches and Mint Leaves

2 Tbsp. olive oil

2 small peaches

4 fillets wild spring salmon,
each 5 oz.

2 shallots, finely sliced

2 small carrots, julienned

1 rib celery, julienned

8 mint leaves

6 Tbsp. dry white wine

"EN PAPILLOTE" is food served in an envelope of paper (or foil) that cooks in its own juices. *Serves 4*

Preheat the oven to 400°F. Cut 4 pieces of parchment paper, each 15 × 18 inches. Fold each sheet along its width, to create a rectangle 15 x 9 inches. Using scissors, round off the 2 unfolded corners. Unfold each sheet, then brush the middle with oil. Be sure to leave a ½-inch border unoiled around the edges.

Fill a bowl with ice water. Fill a saucepan with water and bring to a boil on high heat. Add peaches and blanch for 15 seconds, then use a slotted spoon to transfer them to the bowl of ice water. Let cool, then drain and remove the skins. Remove the pits and cut into slices ½-inch thick.

Season salmon with salt and pepper. Place a salmon fillet on the bottom half of each piece of parchment paper. Top each fillet with a quarter of the peaches, a quarter of the shallots, a quarter of the carrots, a quarter of the celery and 2 mint leaves. Drizzle with wine.

Fold the top half of the parchment paper over the salmon to cover it. Starting at one end of the crease, fold the open edges together snugly, overlapping them firmly as you work your way around to the other end of the crease. Fold the last overlaps several times to seal the package. Repeat with the remaining 3 fillets. Place the parcels on a cookie sheet and bake in the oven for 8 minutes for each 1 inch of thickness of the salmon.

TO SERVE: Place a parcel on each plate. Using scissors, cut open each parcel just below the sealed edge. Carefully roll back the parchment paper to reveal the fish. Be careful not to burn yourself with the steam.

WINE: The more delicate texture from the papillote preparation suits unoaked Chardonnay, either Township 7, with its lemon acidity, or crisp Domaine Combret.

Vacherin with Blood Orange Sorbet
and Grand Marnier Ganache

VACHERIN IS an iced dessert made from meringue, fruit and ice cream, so called because it looks like a round of Vacherin cheese. You can make the genoise or sponge cake and the meringues, but life will be easier if you purchase them at a good bakery. But if you have an ice-cream maker do try to make this sorbet instead of buying one, as the colour and flavour of the blood oranges make this a special dish. If you're feeling flush, use sparkling wine or Champagne instead of the white wine. *Serves 4*

SORBET: Place sugar and water in a saucepan on medium heat. Stir well and bring to a boil. Remove from the heat and let cool. You will be using 1 cup of this sugar syrup (the rest will keep in an airtight container in the refrigerator for up to 6 months).

Combine 1 cup of the sugar syrup, orange juice and wine in a bowl. Refrigerate for about 2 hours. Transfer to an ice-cream maker and process according to the manufacturer's instructions. Freeze sorbet for 4 hours before serving.

GANACHE: Place chocolate and butter in a bowl. Place cream in a saucepan on medium heat. Bring to a boil and pour over chocolate and butter. Let sit for 1 minute, then stir until smooth. Slowly stir in Grand Marnier.

CREAM: Whip cream, sugar and vanilla in an electric mixer until stiff peaks form. Transfer to a bowl and refrigerate until needed.

ORANGE SYRUP: Fill a saucepan with water and bring to a boil on high heat. Blanch zest for 2 minutes, then drain and pat dry with paper towels.

Place orange zest, orange juice and sugar in a saucepan on medium-high heat. Stir until sugar dissolves. Add Grand Marnier, then turn down the heat to low and simmer for about 5 minutes, until the mixture is syrupy. *continued overleaf >*

SORBET
1 cup sugar

1 cup water

1½ cups blood orange juice (about 6 to 8 oranges)

½ cup dry white wine

GANACHE
1 cup dark chocolate, in pieces

4 Tbsp. unsalted butter

6 Tbsp. whipping cream

2 Tbsp. Grand Marnier

CREAM
1½ cups whipping cream

2 Tbsp. sugar

1 tsp. vanilla extract

Chocolate shavings for garnish (optional)

ORANGE SYRUP
3 blood oranges, zest of, julienned

2 oranges, juice of

2 Tbsp. sugar

¼ cup Grand Marnier

CAKE

4 disks genoise or sponge cake, 2½ inches in diameter, ½-inch thick

4 disks dry meringue, 2½ inches in diameter, 1½-inches thick

TO ASSEMBLE: Spread ¾ inch of the ganache on each piece of cake and top with a scoop of sorbet. Cover the sorbet with a meringue, pressing down lightly. Use a small knife to tidy up the sides of the vacherins, if necessary.

Place the vacherins on a cookie sheet and freeze for 20 minutes. Remove from the freezer and transfer to individual plates.

Place the whipped cream in a piping bag fitted with a star tip, then pipe over and around each vacherin. Freeze the decorated vacherins for 20 minutes.

TO SERVE: Allow the vacherins to thaw for 5 to 10 minutes. Use a knife dipped in hot water to cut a quarter wedge out of each vacherin. Turn the cut pieces so that the cut side is showing. Drizzle with the orange syrup and sprinkle with a few chocolate shavings (optional).

WINE: The sweet meringue finds friendly company with the Peller Estates Trinity Icewine Founder's Series from the Okanagan Valley.

Vacherin with Blood Orange Sorbet and Grand Marnier Ganache

Smoked Tuna Broth with Seared Tuna

KOMBU IS a flavourful dried kelp that is often covered with a powdery white substance. Lightly brush off some of this powder before using the kombu. Mirin is a sweet rice wine. Both of these ingredients are available in Japanese specialty stores. *Serves 4*

Place water, kombu, ginger and dried mushrooms in a saucepan on medium heat. (Be sure to start with cold water to make a clear broth.) Bring to a boil and remove from the heat immediately. Add bonito flakes, cover and let steep for 20 minutes.

Strain through a fine-mesh sieve and discard solids. (Do not press the solids or the broth will be cloudy.) Gently stir in soy sauce, mirin, vinegar and sugar. (If not using immediately, cool to room temperature and refrigerate. Will keep in the refrigerator, covered, for up to 4 days, or frozen for up to 3 months.)

Reheat broth in a saucepan on medium heat. Add noodles and fresh mushrooms, then cook until piping hot.

Season tuna with sea salt and a generous amount of freshly cracked black pepper. Heat a dry nonstick frying pan on medium-high heat. Sear tuna on one side for 30 to 40 seconds, then turn over and sear for 30 to 40 seconds. Transfer to a warmed plate and cut into slices ¾-inch thick.

TO SERVE: Ladle noodles, mushrooms and broth into individual bowls and top with warm tuna slices.

WINE: Pair the tuna with either a white—Sandhill's fresh Pinot Blanc, or a red—the unique Lake Breeze Pinotage.

8½ cups cold water

1 stick kombu, 5 inches long

1-inch piece fresh ginger, sliced

4 dried shiitake mushrooms

2 oz. bonito flakes

1½ cups light soy sauce

½ cup mirin

3 Tbsp. + 2 tsp. Japanese seasoned rice vinegar

3 Tbsp. sugar

8 oz. soba noodles, cooked as directed on package and cooled

½ cup (about 4) fresh shiitake mushrooms, destemmed and sliced

1 lb. albacore or Ahi tuna, in 4 equal portions

Warm Belgian Chocolate Cake

1 cup unsalted butter, soft

8 oz. good-quality semi-sweet
dark chocolate

2 Tbsp. espresso or
strong dark coffee

½ cup white bread flour

½ cup sugar

Pinch of salt

4 eggs

4 egg yolks

SERVE THIS CAKE on its own or with a small scoop of good-quality vanilla or hazelnut ice cream. *Serves 6*

Preheat the oven to 400°F. Grease six ½-cup ramekins.

Place butter and chocolate in a stainless steel bowl over a saucepan of hot (not boiling) water on lowest heat. Stir frequently with a heat-resistant rubber spatula, until butter and chocolate are melted. Stir in coffee. Remove from the heat and let cool to luke-warm.

Combine flour, sugar and salt in a bowl. Whisk dry ingredients into chocolate mixture, bit by bit, until well combined. Whisk in eggs and egg yolks, one at a time, until completely mixed each time. Let batter rest for 5 minutes.

Stir batter with a wooden spoon or spatula, then fill ramekins three-quarters full. Bake in the oven for about 6 minutes, until the cake is firmly set on the outside but warm and liquid in the centre. Allow to rest for 1 minute. Run a thin sharp knife around the edge of each cake.

TO SERVE: Gently unmould a warm cake onto each plate.

WINE: Sip Venturi-Schulze Brandenburg No. 3 dessert wine with its caramel-coffee notes.

{ ARAXI: *james walt* }

Warm Belgian Chocolate Cake

{ ARIA AT THE WESTIN GRAND: *david foot* }

Shrimp and Crab Salad with Grapefruit Vinaigrette

Shrimp and Crab Salad with Grapefruit Vinaigrette

USE A WELL-WASHED empty tuna can with both ends removed as a shaper for the shrimp mixture and later to cut out rounds of aspic. For an alternate presentation, cut the aspic into small diamond shapes and arrange them around the plate. The vinaigrette has no oil on purpose. *Serves 4*

ASPIC: Place ¼ cup of the fish stock in a bowl. Add the gelatine and mix well.

Place the remaining fish stock in a saucepan on medium heat and bring to a boil. Season with salt and pepper. Pour into the gelatine mixture, stirring until the gelatine is dissolved. Pour into a 9 × 13-inch baking pan to a depth of about ⅛ inch, then refrigerate on a level shelf for about 1 hour, until set.

VINAIGRETTE: Whisk together grapefruit juice, sugar and vinegar in a bowl.

SALAD: Combine shrimp, crab and mayonnaise in a bowl. Mix well.

TO SERVE: Set a clean tuna can in the middle of a plate. Spoon the seafood mixture into the can, then remove the can carefully. Repeat this process on the 3 other plates. Clean the tuna can and use it to cut out 4 circles of aspic and place one on each round of seafood. Top with a small tuft of sunflower sprouts, leaving some of the aspic exposed so that it adds sparkle to the dish. Drizzle with some of the vinaigrette.

WINE: Grapefruit and seafood pair well with the citrus and grapefruit essences of Chalet Estate Vineyard Ortega.

ASPIC
2 cups fish stock or chicken stock

2 envelopes Knox gelatine powder

VINAIGRETTE
1 grapefruit, juice of

2 Tbsp. sugar

2 Tbsp. rice vinegar

SALAD
6 oz. cooked baby shrimp

6 oz. cooked Dungeness crabmeat

2 Tbsp. mayonnaise

¼ cup sunflower sprouts or other micro greens

Pecan and Ginger Free-range Chicken

4 Tbsp. coarsely chopped
toasted pecans

2 tsp. finely chopped
fresh ginger

1 cup rolled oats

4 Tbsp. butter,
room temperature

⅛ tsp. nutmeg

4 free-range chicken breast
halves, boneless, skin on

1 Tbsp. vegetable oil

BE SURE TO USE regular rolled oats in this recipe, because the quick or instant varieties will become soggy. Garnish each plate with cooked vegetables. *Serves 4*

To make the topping, place pecans, ginger, oats, butter and nutmeg in a bowl. Season with salt and pepper, then mix until crumbly. Refrigerate for 1 hour.

Preheat the oven to 350°F. Season chicken with salt and pepper. Heat oil in an ovenproof frying pan on medium-high heat. Sear chicken, skin side down, for about 5 minutes, until golden. Turn over chicken and roast in the oven for 15 minutes.

Remove from the oven. Spread the pecan topping over the browned, crispy skin of the chicken and pat it down. Return to oven and bake for 10 minutes, until chicken is done. (The juices will run clear.)

TO SERVE: Make 3 or 4 diagonal cuts through each breast half and fan out. Place one breast half on each plate.

WINE: Match the ginger and pecans with Blasted Church Vineyard Merlot–Cabernet Sauvignon (with a dash of Pinot Noir).

Roasted Pork Loin with Potato Purée and Green Beans

MARINADE

3 Tbsp. molasses

1 ½-inch piece grated
fresh ginger

½ cup ketchup

3 cloves garlic, crushed

1 chili pepper, deseeded
and chopped

1 lime, zest and juice of

1 cup fresh cilantro leaves,
roughly chopped

PORK

4 lbs. (4 to 5 ribs) pork centre
loin in one piece, skin off

1½ cups water
or chicken stock

VEGETABLES

1 lb. green beans, trimmed

4 Yukon Gold potatoes,
in large cubes

⅓ cup milk or whipping cream

4 Tbsp. butter

2 Tbsp. finely chopped
fresh parsley

1 Tbsp. butter or olive oil

ASK THE BUTCHER to take the meat off the bone, tie the roast and then tie the roast back on to the bone. The bone cushions the meat as it roasts and adds additional flavour to the pan juices. *Serves 6*

MARINADE: Place all the ingredients in a food processor and purée roughly. Pour into a large resealable plastic freezer bag. Add pork, seal the bag and turn to coat with the marinade. Place the bag in a bowl and marinate pork in the refrigerator for 24 hours, turning it every 6 hours.

PORK: Preheat the oven to 475°F. Remove pork from the bag and discard marinade.

Gently shake off excess marinade from pork and place in a roasting pan. Sear in the oven for 15 minutes to seal in juices. Turn down the oven to 350°F and roast for 35 minutes, until a meat thermometer reads 140°F. Cook for a few minutes more, until the meat thermometer reads 160°F for medium or 170°F for well done. Remove from the oven and transfer to a serving platter. Save the pan. Let pork rest for 10 minutes before carving.

Skim off and discard excess fat from the reserved roasting pan. Add water and deglaze the pan on medium heat. Season with salt and pepper and cook until pan juices are slightly syrupy. Strain through a fine-mesh sieve and discard solids. Save the strained pan juices.

VEGETABLES: Fill a large bowl with ice water. Bring a large pot of salted water to a boil. Plunge green beans into the boiling water and cook until slightly crunchy, about 4 minutes. Drop green beans into the ice water and let cool for 5 minutes, then drain and pat dry.

Place potatoes in a saucepan and cover with salted cold water. Cover with a lid, bring to a boil on medium heat and simmer until soft, about 12 minutes. Drain.

In a clean saucepan, scald milk and the 4 Tbsp. of butter on medium heat. Remove from the heat.

Mash potatoes or put them through a ricer. Slowly add scalded milk, whisking gently to incorporate. Season with salt, pepper and parsley.

Just before serving, heat the 1 Tbsp. of butter in a frying pan on medium heat. Add green beans and season with salt and pepper. Cook green beans, turning them from side to side with tongs, for 2 to 3 minutes, until done.

TO SERVE: Place a spoonful of potato purée in the centre of each plate, then top with a neat row of green beans and 3 thick slices of roasted pork loin. Drizzle with pan juices.

WINE: Savour this dish with a fruity Blue Mountain Gamay Noir.

Whole Roast Chicken on Potato Slices
with Spiced Apple Relish

CHICKEN

5 to 6 lbs. free-range roasting
chicken or small turkey

1 lemon, in wedges

3 cloves garlic, roughly chopped

2 sprigs fresh thyme

2 sprigs fresh rosemary

2 sprigs fresh marjoram

2 tsp. chopped fresh thyme

2 tsp. chopped fresh rosemary

2 tsp. chopped fresh marjoram

3 Tbsp. Dijon mustard

1 large russet potato,
in 1-inch slices

¾ cup water

1½ cups water or chicken stock

1 to 2 Tbsp. unsalted butter

RELISH

1 onion, finely chopped

4 Granny Smith apples, peeled,
cored and in ⅓-inch dice

1 red chili pepper, finely chopped

Small bunch cilantro, chopped

1-inch piece fresh ginger, grated

½ cup brown sugar

¼ cup cider vinegar

1 cinnamon stick

1 cup cranberries (optional)

½ cup chopped toasted
pecans (optional)

A GOOD ROAST CHICKEN makes a delicious dinner. Seasoning the bird with mustard and herbs enhances the flavour. *Serves 6*

CHICKEN: Preheat the oven to 450°F.

Place chicken on a cutting board. Use your fingers to pull the skin away from the neck to expose the Y-shaped wishbone. Use a sharp knife to cut through the flesh on each side of the wishbone in order to remove it (this will make it easier to slice after it is cooked). Wipe the chicken inside and out with paper towels.

Place lemon, garlic and sprigs of thyme, rosemary and marjoram inside the bird. Close the cavity with skewers and truss the chicken with kitchen string.

Combine chopped thyme, rosemary and marjoram in a bowl. Brush mustard onto the chicken and sprinkle with chopped herbs. (The chicken may be prepared to this point then refrigerated, covered loosely with plastic wrap to prevent the mustard from drying out, for up to 12 hours.)

Place potato slices in a large roasting pan, set the chicken on top and add the ¾ cup of water. Roast in the oven for 15 minutes. Turn down the heat to 375°F and cook for about 1 hour, basting with pan juices every 15 minutes, until a meat thermometer inserted into the thickest part of the thigh reads 180°F.

Remove from the oven. Transfer chicken and potatoes to a platter and let rest for 5 to 10 minutes before carving. Pour pan juices into a saucepan, then skim off and discard fat. Save the roasting pan.

Add the 1½ cups of water and deglaze the reserved roasting pan. Strain into the saucepan of pan juices and discard any solids. Cook on high heat for 7 to 8 minutes, until reduced to about half. Season with salt and pepper. Keep warm. Just before serving, whisk in butter.

RELISH: Place onion, apples, chili pepper, cilantro, ginger, sugar, vinegar and cinnamon stick in a saucepan and bring to a boil on medium heat. Turn down the heat to low and simmer for 20 to 30 minutes, until relish begins to thicken. Add cranberries (optional) and cook for 10 minutes, until relish is thick. Remove and discard cinnamon stick. Just before serving, sprinkle with toasted pecans (optional).

TO SERVE: Carve the chicken into ⅓-inch thick slices and place 3 on each plate. Serve the pan juices in a sauceboat and the relish in a bowl on the side.

WINE: New World–style Hillside Estate Mosaic Reserve uses the five Bordeaux grapes, showing lovely cherries, cedar and chocolate to set off this dish.

{ *murray bancroft* }

Citrus-cured Wild Salmon with Blood Orange Vodka

Citrus-cured Wild Salmon

with Blood Orange Vodka

BEGIN PREPARING the salmon the week before you plan to serve it, because it must marinate for several days. Serve with slices of bread and dollops of crème fraîche.

For an authentic Scandinavian brunch buffet, serve either blood orange–flavoured or unflavoured vodka with this dish. *Serves 12 to 16*

BLOOD ORANGE VODKA: Place vodka, oranges, cinnamon and star anise in a glass bowl. Save the vodka bottle. Cover the bowl tightly with plastic wrap and refrigerate for 1 to 2 days.

Strain through a fine-mesh sieve into the reserved vodka bottle. Store in the freezer indefinitely.

SALMON: Combine ¼ cup of the sugar and ¼ cup of the sea salt in a bowl. Place salmon, skin side down, in a large casserole dish. Rub sugar mixture over the entire surface of salmon. Cover the dish tightly with plastic wrap and refrigerate for 2 days.

Unwrap salmon, then sprinkle with the remaining sugar and sea salt, basil, mint, lemon juice and zest, coriander seeds and vodka. Wrap salmon tightly in plastic wrap (or cover salmon with a layer of plastic wrap, then cover dish tightly with plastic wrap). Refrigerate for 3 to 4 days.

Unwrap salmon, then rinse under cold running water. Pat dry with paper towels.

TO SERVE: Thinly slice salmon and arrange on a serving platter.

WINE: Serve with rounds of blood orange vodka, or Adora in Summerland's "Elements" Barrel Fermented Pinot Gris or spicy exotic Decorus White.

BLOOD ORANGE VODKA

26-oz. bottle vodka

2 to 3 blood oranges, sliced

1 stick cinnamon

2 pieces star anise

SALMON

¼ cup + 2 Tbsp. brown sugar

¼ cup + 2 Tbsp. sea salt

1 fillet wild sockeye salmon, skin on, 3 to 4 lbs.

1 bunch Thai basil, cut in chiffonade

1 bunch mint, cut in chiffonade

1 lemon, zest and juice of

1 to 2 tsp. crushed coriander seeds

3 oz. blood orange vodka

Bonfire Wild Sockeye Salmon with Waldorf Salad

AÏOLI

¾ cup mayonnaise

½ cup shiro miso

1 lemon, zest of

SALAD

½ cup wild rice, rinsed under cold running water

1½ cups chicken stock, preferably homemade

2 large Granny Smith apples

2 Tbsp. fresh lemon juice

1 cup celeriac, julienned

¼ cup walnut pieces, lightly toasted

Small handful of fresh Italian flat-leaf parsley, leaves only

SALMON

8 sprigs fresh rosemary

8 sprigs fresh thyme

8 sprigs fresh oregano

4 fillets fresh wild sockeye salmon, each 6 oz.

4 Tbsp. olive oil

1 Tbsp. fresh lemon juice for garnish

1 Tbsp. extra-virgin olive oil for garnish

MISO IS A HIGH-PROTEIN SEASONING made from soybeans, cultured rice, salt and water. It's used mainly in soups, sauces, dips and dressings. Look for miso in the refrigerator at your favourite health food or Asian specialty store. *Serves 4*

AÏOLI: Place mayonnaise, miso, lemon zest, salt and freshly ground white pepper in a food processor and blend until smooth.

SALAD: Place rice and stock in a saucepan on medium-high heat and bring to a boil. Cover with a lid, then turn down the heat to low and cook without stirring for 35 minutes, until very tender. (If rice is not tender and looks dry, add a bit more water and cook for a little longer.) Drain, if necessary, and discard liquid. Season with a little salt and let cool.

Peel, core and thinly slice apples, then place in a bowl and toss with 1 Tbsp. of the lemon juice to prevent them from turning brown. Place celeriac in another bowl and toss with the remaining lemon juice.

In a bowl, combine wild rice, apples, celeriac, walnuts and parsley. Add enough aïoli to lightly bind the salad.

SALMON: Place rosemary, thyme and oregano on a paper towel and set in a warm place to dry overnight.

Preheat a barbecue to medium-high. Brush each salmon fillet with oil to lightly coat, then season with salt and freshly ground white pepper.

Place dried herbs in the bottom part of a hinged rectangular barbecue basket and place on the grill. When the herbs begin to smoke lightly, place salmon on top of them, pressing down gently so the fish absorbs some of the herb flavour. Invert an ovenproof pan or a clay pot over salmon and cook on one side only for 7 to 8 minutes, until medium-rare.

TO SERVE: Divide salad among individual plates. Top each with a hot salmon fillet, then garnish with a drizzle of lemon juice and a drizzle of olive oil. Serve any additional aïoli in a bowl on the side.

WINE: Serve with Nk'Mip Cellars' full mineral-baked apple Qwam Qwmt ("achieving excellence") Chardonnay from Osoyoos, by North America's first Aboriginal-owned and -operated winery.

Candied Apple Tart

PUFF PASTRY is sold either fresh or frozen. The frozen variety is easier to find, but many bakeries will sell you fresh puff pastry dough if you phone ahead. You will need 1 pound.

Serve this dish with vanilla ice cream augmented with Scotch. Several hours before serving, slightly soften the ice cream, stir in 2 Tbsp. Scotch, then refreeze the mixture. *Serves 6*

SUGAR GLASS: Cover a cutting board with a sheet of parchment paper.

Melt sugar and water in a saucepan on medium-high heat. Cook, without stirring, for about 10 minutes, until sugar is a light caramel colour. (Stirring may cause sugar to crystallize before it turns to caramel.) Stir in butter.

Use a metal spatula to spread caramel very thinly on the parchment paper. Let cool until hard. Break sugar glass into pieces roughly 3 × 3 inches. Store in an airtight container indefinitely.

APPLESAUCE: Place butter in a saucepan on medium heat and cook for about 3 minutes, until brown. Add cardamom and cinnamon sticks. Stir in honey and add apples. Turn down the heat to low and simmer for 30 minutes, until applesauce is thick. Remove and discard cinnamon sticks.

FILLING: Place sugar in a saucepan on medium heat and cook, swirling the pan constantly, not stirring, until lightly caramelized. Slowly stir in water, then add lemon. Bring to a boil, then turn down the heat to low and simmer for 5 minutes, until the caramelized sugar has melted. Remove and discard the lemon slices. Gently stir apple slices into this syrup and poach for 5 minutes, until slightly tender. Remove from the heat and let cool. Use a slotted spoon to transfer apple slices to a clean plate. Reserve the syrup in an airtight container in the fridge for up to 7 days for another use. *continued overleaf >*

SUGAR GLASS
½ cup sugar

2 tsp. water

2 Tbsp. butter

APPLESAUCE
2 Tbsp. butter

1 tsp. ground toasted cardamom seeds

2 cinnamon sticks, broken in half

2 Tbsp. wildflower honey

6 large Golden Delicious apples, peeled, cored and in 1-inch dice

FILLING
2 cups sugar

6 cups water

1 lemon, in ½-inch slices

6 large Granny Smith apples, peeled, cored, in ½-inch lengthwise slices

PASTRY

14 oz. frozen puff pastry, thawed

¼ tsp. ground cinnamon

1 tsp. icing sugar

1 Tbsp. butter, melted

PASTRY: Preheat the oven to 350°F. Grease six 4-inch tart pans, with removable bottoms, if you have them.

Roll out puff pastry on a lightly floured surface to a thickness of ⅛ inch. Cut pastry into six 5 to 6-inch circles and press one into each tart pan.

TO ASSEMBLE: Place ⅓ cup of applesauce into each tart pan. Arrange apple slices in a spiral pattern over the applesauce, then dust with ground cinnamon and icing sugar.

Bake in the oven for 25 minutes. Brush the top of each tart with melted butter, then bake for about 5 minutes, until apples are tender and the pastry is golden. Remove from the oven but leave the oven on.

TO SERVE: Run a knife around the edge of the puff pastry, then gently unmould the tarts onto a cookie sheet. Place a piece of sugar glass on each tart. Warm in the oven for 3 minutes. The glass will melt over the apples, then harden as it cools. It should crunch with a fork. Serve warm on individual plates.

WINE: A good match for Sumac Ridge Pinot Blanc Icewine, with its apple pie and cinnamon statement.

{ BIN 941/942: *gord martin* }

Candied Apple Tart

{ BIS MORENO: *moreno miotto* }

Risotto Porcini

Arrabbiata Sauce

ARRABBIATA MEANS "ANGRY" in Italian. Serve this classic spicy sauce over penne pasta. *Serves 6*

Heat oil in a saucepan on medium heat, then sauté garlic and chili flakes for 5 minutes, until garlic begins to brown. Add puréed tomatoes and cook for 10 to 15 minutes, until slightly thickened. Season to taste with salt and pepper or more chili flakes, if necessary. Stir in the parsley just before serving.

WINE: Try Hainle Vineyards' lower-alcohol fresh organic Pinot Blanc with extended lees aging.

2 Tbsp. extra-virgin olive oil

6 cloves garlic, crushed

1 Tbsp. chili flakes or to taste

32-oz. can whole organic plum tomatoes, undrained and puréed

2 Tbsp. chopped fresh Italian flat-leaf parsley

Risotto Porcini

THIS TASTY RISOTTO RECIPE can be prepared in less than 40 minutes. *Serves 4*

Strain the soaked dried mushrooms through a fine-mesh sieve into a clean bowl. Save the soaking liquid. Squeeze mushrooms dry, then brush away grit and trim off and discard hard edges.

Place rice in a sieve and rinse under cold running water. Drain, then place in a saucepan and just cover with cold water. Bring to a boil on medium-high heat, then turn down the heat to low and simmer for 4 to 5 minutes, until just al dente. Remove from the heat and rinse in a sieve under cold running water until rice is cool. Drain (will keep at room temperature for several hours).

Heat oil in a saucepan on medium-high heat. Sauté mushrooms, onion and garlic for 1 to 2 minutes, until onion is translucent. Stir in rice. Add vermouth, deglaze the pan and cook for 2 minutes. Pour in enough stock to just cover the rice. Bring the rice to a boil and stir in butter. Season with salt and pepper. Cook, stirring constantly, and add the remaining stock ½ cup at a time as liquid is absorbed until rice is creamy. Remove from the heat and stir in Parmesan.

TO SERVE: Divide into individual bowls.

WINE: Italian-style Sandhill three from Burrowing Owl Vineyard.

1 cup dried porcini (cèpes) mushrooms soaked in boiling water for 2 hours

1 cup arborio rice

2 Tbsp. extra-virgin olive oil

¼ onion, finely chopped

1 tsp. finely chopped garlic

4 Tbsp. Noilly Prat or other dry white vermouth

2 cups chicken stock

2 Tbsp. unsalted butter

½ cup grated Parmesan

Five Spice-roasted Duck Breast with Shiitake Mushroom
and Wilted Spinach Salad with Blackberry Balsamic Syrup

SYRUP

½ cup blackberry vinegar

1 cup balsamic vinegar

DUCK AND VEGETABLES

2 duck breast halves, each 8 oz.

1 Tbsp. five-spice powder

1 Tbsp. sesame oil

½ cup shiitake mushrooms, destemmed and sliced

2 cups spinach leaves, destemmed

DUCK BREASTS are available in specialty butcher shops. You can also buy whole ducks, then cut off the breasts. Braise the legs and save the carcass to make stock. *Serves 4*

SYRUP: Place blackberry and balsamic vinegars in a saucepan, then bring to a boil on medium heat. Simmer for about 15 minutes, until reduced to ½ cup. Let cool and refrigerate until needed. Will keep for several weeks in the refrigerator.

DUCK AND VEGETABLES: Preheat the oven to 450°F. Use a sharp knife to score the skin on duck breasts in a diagonal cross-hatch pattern. Season with sea salt and five-spice powder.

Heat an ovenproof frying pan on medium heat. Place duck in pan, skin side down, and sear for 5 minutes, until lightly browned and the skin begins to render its fat. Pour off and discard the accumulated fat. Turn over duck, then roast in the oven for 5 minutes. Turn over again so duck is skin side down, then roast for 5 minutes, until cooked to medium. (The meat will be pink or rosy in the middle.) Remove from the oven and place duck on a cutting board in a warm spot to rest for 5 minutes.

Skim off and discard fat from the roasting pan. Add sesame oil and sauté mushrooms on medium-high heat for 8 to 10 minutes, until lightly caramelized. Add spinach, tossing lightly while cooking for about 2 minutes, until slightly wilted. Season to taste with salt and pepper.

TO SERVE: Divide spinach-mushroom salad among individual plates. Slice each duck breast at a 45-degree angle into 6 slices, and place 3 on each serving. Drizzle with blackberry-balsamic syrup.

WINE: A lovely dish with Inniskillin's smoky cherry and raspberry Dark Horse Estate Vineyard Pinot Noir from the Okanagan Valley.

Slow-cooked Lamb Shoulder

with Pan-roasted Vegetables

SLOW-COOKED MEAT is such a delight. Once it's in the oven, you can forget about it for a few hours, and the meat becomes so tender that it just pulls away from the bone. Shoulder cuts are best for slow-cooking recipes, because they require longer cooking times and have lots of flavour, a bonus with such an economical cut of meat. This dish can be cooked a day ahead; remove and discard any hardened fat, then reheat gently. *Serves 6*

Preheat the oven to 450°F. Grind together sea salt, mustard seeds and peppercorns with a mortar and pestle or in an electric spice mill. Rub lamb all over with olive oil, garlic and ground spices.

Combine onions, carrots, parsnips and turnips in a roasting pan, then place lamb on top. Roast in the oven for about 45 minutes, until meat is well coloured. Remove from oven and cover the pan tightly with aluminum foil, shiny side in. Turn down the oven to 350°F and roast meat for about 2 hours, until it is fully cooked and pulls away from the bone.

Transfer meat to a warmed platter and let rest for 15 to 20 minutes. Strain liquid from vegetables into a clean bowl, then skim off and discard fat. Return the liquid to the vegetables.

TO SERVE: Carve lamb into slices ¾-inch thick and place 3 slices on each plate. Arrange some vegetables and juice beside the lamb.

WINE: Mission Hill's complex Oculus has matching notes of bell pepper, cedar and smoky truffles.

1 Tbsp. sea salt

1 tsp. mustard seeds

1 tsp. black peppercorns

3½ lbs. lamb shoulder, whole, bone in

2 Tbsp. olive oil

1 tsp. minced garlic

1 cup onions, in 1-inch dice

2 cups carrots, in 1-inch dice

1 cup parsnips, in 1-inch dice

1 cup turnips, in 1-inch dice

Hazelnut Spice Cake

with Dried Fruit and Late-harvest Riesling Compote

COMPOTE

1 cup dried fruit

1 cup late-harvest Riesling or other late-harvest wine

½ cup water

½ cup honey

1 cinnamon stick

1 star anise

CAKE

½ cup hazelnuts

1¼ cups all-purpose flour, preferably unbleached

1 tsp. baking powder

½ tsp. baking soda

½ tsp. salt

Pinch of nutmeg

Pinch of cinnamon

Pinch of cardamom

½ cup butter

½ cup brown sugar

2 eggs

½ cup buttermilk

¼ cup dark rum

CHERRIES, APRICOTS AND FIGS are especially good in this compote. You can use just one of these fruits, or a combination, or experiment with fruits of your own choosing. Make the compote a day ahead to allow its flavour to develop. You can also make the cakes ahead of time, or you can bake the batter in an 8-inch cake pan instead of individual ramekins. Warm the pre-made cakes in a microwave oven and serve with a scoop of vanilla ice cream. *Serves 6*

COMPOTE: Roughly slice large fruits, such as apricots or figs. Leave cherries whole.

Place wine, water, honey, cinnamon and star anise in a saucepan on medium heat. Once the mixture simmers, add dried fruit. Cover with a lid, then simmer for 10 minutes. Remove from the heat, leave covered and let cool. Remove and discard cinnamon and star anise. Refrigerate until needed, up to 7 days.

CAKE: Preheat the oven to 350°F. Grease and flour six ½-cup ramekins.

Place hazelnuts on a cookie sheet and toast in the oven for 5 to 10 minutes, until fragrant and golden. Transfer to a clean tea towel, then rub them gently to remove the skins. Let cool.

Combine hazelnuts, flour, baking powder, baking soda, salt, nutmeg, cinnamon and cardamom in a food processor. Pulse until the nuts are finely ground.

Cream butter and sugar in an electric mixer until light and fluffy. Add eggs, one at a time, mixing well after each addition. Lightly mix in buttermilk and rum. Add the dry ingredients and mix batter well.

Pour batter into the ramekins. Bake in the oven for 25 to 30 minutes, until a toothpick inserted into the centre of the cakes comes out clean.

TO SERVE: Dip the bottom of the ramekins in hot water. Run a knife around the edge of the cakes, then gently unmould them. Place a warm cake on each plate and spoon some compote on top.

WINE: Try the Hester Creek Late Harvest Trebbiano Reserve instead of a Vin Santo.

{ BISHOP'S: *dennis green & john bishop* }

Hazelnut Spice Cake with Dried Fruit and Late-harvest Riesling Compote

{ BISTRO PASTIS: *john blakeley* }

Les Moules et les Poivrons

Les Moules et les Poivrons
(Mussels and Sweet Peppers)

WE USE MUSSELS from Saltspring Island. Serve this dish with a tossed green salad and a loaf of crusty bread for a light meal. *Serves 4*

HERB BUTTER: Blend butter, herbs and lemon juice in a food processor. Scrape herb butter onto a large piece of plastic wrap and form into a long cylinder, using the wrap to help shape it as you roll. Twist the ends of the plastic wrap to close them, then refrigerate until butter is chilled and hard.

PIPERADE: Heat oil in a saucepan on medium heat. Sauté red and yellow bell peppers for about 15 minutes, until tender. Add shallot and cook for 1 minute. Add vinegar and deglaze, then cook sauce for about 5 minutes, until it is almost dry. Season with salt and pepper. Refrigerate until needed, up to 1 day.

MUSSELS AND SAUCE: Tap mussels lightly with a knife and discard any that remain open. Place mussels, wine, vinegar, vermouth, shallot, bay leaf, thyme and garlic in a heavy saucepan on high heat. Cover with a lid and cook for about 3 minutes, or just until mussels open. Strain the cooking liquid into another saucepan and save. Discard any mussels that have not opened. Remove the meat from the shells. Transfer the mussel meat and 36 of the best shell halves to a clean bowl and refrigerate.

TO ASSEMBLE: Preheat the broiler.

Place the reserved mussel cooking liquid in a saucepan on high heat and cook until the liquid is almost dry. Whisk in ¼ cup of the chilled herb butter to make a sauce.

Spread out the mussel shells on a cookie sheet. Place a spoonful of piperade in each shell, then top with a mussel. Add a dab of the remaining herb butter and sprinkle with bread crumbs. Broil for 1 to minutes, until butter melts and crumbs brown.

TO SERVE: Divide the broiled mussels among individual plates and drizzle with warm sauce.

WINE: The peach-noted Jackson-Triggs Proprietors' Reserve Viognier from Bull Pine Vineyard is ideal.

HERB BUTTER
⅓ cup butter at room temperature
Small handful of mixed fresh herbs (chives, dill, parsley), roughly chopped
½ lemon, juice of

PIPERADE
2 tsp. olive oil
1 red bell pepper, finely diced
1 yellow bell pepper, finely diced
1 shallot, finely diced
1 Tbsp. white wine vinegar

MUSSELS AND SAUCE
3 dozen mussels, well scrubbed, beards removed
⅞ cup dry white wine
¼ cup white wine vinegar
¼ cup dry white vermouth
1 shallot, finely chopped
1 bay leaf
1 large sprig thyme
1 clove garlic, crushed
2 Tbsp. bread crumbs

Seared Halibut with Wild Rice Pilaf

and Lemon-Shallot Sauce

WILD RICE PILAF

1 Tbsp. unsalted butter

¼ onion, in ¼-inch dice

4 wild mushrooms (chanterelles, morels or shiitakes), sliced

3 Tbsp. diced celery

3 Tbsp. diced carrot

1 cup wild rice

3 cups chicken stock, hot

½ tsp. salt

1 bay leaf

1 large sprig thyme

HALIBUT AND BOK CHOY

4 fillets halibut, each 5 oz.

2 Tbsp. olive oil

1 Tbsp. butter

4 baby bok choy, split lengthwise and hard ends removed

SAUCE

1 large shallot, chopped

½ cup chicken stock

7 Tbsp. cold unsalted butter, cubed

½ lemon, juice of, or to taste

FOR VARIETY, serve the wild rice pilaf as a cold salad. Let the rice cool for several hours in the refrigerator, then season with salt, pepper and 1 to 2 Tbsp. of vinaigrette. *Serves 4*

WILD RICE PILAF: Preheat the oven to 400°F.

Melt butter in an ovenproof frying pan on medium-high heat. Sauté onion, mushrooms, celery and carrot for about 10 minutes, until tender. Add wild rice and stir to coat the grains with butter. Stir in stock and salt, then add bay leaf and thyme. Cover with a lid and bake in the oven for about 40 minutes, until rice is cooked. Add more stock, if necessary, to complete cooking.

HALIBUT AND BOK CHOY: Preheat the oven to oven to 400°F. Pat halibut dry with paper towels, then season on both sides with salt and pepper. Heat oil in an ovenproof frying pan and sear halibut for 3 minutes, until crisp and brown. Turn over halibut, then roast in the oven for about 3 minutes, until flesh is just barely opaque. Remove from the oven and let cool for 2 minutes (fish will continue to cook).

Melt butter in a clean frying pan on medium-high heat. Quickly sear bok choy for about 2 minutes, until crisp and tender.

SAUCE: Place shallot and stock in a small saucepan on medium heat and cook for about 5 minutes, until just below boiling. Whisk in butter, one cube at a time. Stir in lemon juice, then season with salt and pepper. The sauce should be light, lemony and frothy. If it is too thick, add a little more stock.

TO SERVE: Place pilaf in the bottom of large serving bowl. Top with the halibut, arrange the bok choy around the fish, then drizzle with sauce.

WINE: Fish-friendly Mission Hill Reserve Chardonnay has bold toasty oak balanced with crisp, refreshing mineral acidity.

Crème Caramel au Chocolat

EVERY PARIS BISTRO serves crème caramel—but not like this version, which is enriched with the addition of bittersweet chocolate and fresh raspberries. *Serves 6*

CARAMEL: Lightly grease six ½-cup ramekins with the butter. Melt sugar in a heavy saucepan on medium heat. Cook, without stirring, for 10 to 12 minutes, until sugar turns a medium caramel colour. (Do not stir or sugar may crystallize before it turns to caramel.) Pour ⅓ inch of caramel into the bottom of each ramekin. Refrigerate while you make the custard.

CUSTARD: Preheat the oven to 350°F.

Combine milk and chocolate in a stainless steel bowl placed over a saucepan of hot water on medium-low heat. Mix gently with a wooden spoon for about 15 minutes, until chocolate is melted and milk almost comes to a boil. Be careful not to burn the chocolate. Remove from the heat and stir until smooth.

In a bowl, whisk together sugar, eggs and egg yolks. Slowly add the chocolate mixture, whisking constantly. (A damp cloth placed under the bowl will help keep the bowl steady while you whisk.) Strain through a sieve over the caramel in the ramekins. Top each one with a raspberry.

Set the ramekins in a large roasting pan and add enough hot water to reach halfway up the sides of the dishes. Bake in the oven for about 30 minutes. Gently shake the ramekins, and if the custard jiggles slightly, it is done. Remove the ramekins from the roasting pan, let cool, then refrigerate for 2 hours.

TO SERVE: Dip the bottom of each ramekin in warm water. Run a knife around the edge of the custard, then place a plate on top of the ramekin and invert both the plate and the ramekin. Remove the ramekin. The caramel will flow over the custard. Repeat for each ramekin, then garnish each plate with a dollop of whipped cream and a raspberry.

WINE: Serve with a "Hearth" port-style from Alderlea, or a Blue Grouse Black Muscat, both from Vancouver Island.

CARAMEL

1 Tbsp. butter

1⅓ cups sugar

CUSTARD

2 cups milk

4 oz. bittersweet chocolate, chopped

½ cup sugar

2 eggs

4 egg yolks

12 fresh raspberries

½ cup whipped cream for garnish

Shrimp and Basil-crusted Red Snapper
with Olive-braised Fennel

FENNEL

2 bulbs fennel

1 Tbsp. + 2 tsp. olive oil

24 small organic
green olives, pitted

2 Roma tomatoes,
roughly chopped

4 cloves garlic, chopped

3 large shallots, chopped

2 sprigs fresh thyme

1 bay leaf

1 cup dry crisp Chardonnay
(not a fruity style)

3 cups chicken stock or water

2 tsp. coriander seeds

½ lemon, juice of

2 Tbsp. chopped fresh parsley

SNAPPER

4 oz. fresh raw side-striped
shrimp meat or local prawns,
finely chopped

4 Tbsp. unsalted butter, softened

4 Tbsp. chopped fresh basil

½ cup dry bread crumbs

4 tsp. chopped toasted pine nuts

¼ tsp. puréed garlic

4 fillets fresh red snapper,
each 5 oz.

½ cup dry crisp white wine

Extra-virgin olive oil for garnish

FOR A CRUNCHY CRUST, use panko bread crumbs (sold in Japanese food stores) instead of dry bread crumbs to coat the snapper. *Serves 4*

FENNEL: Preheat the oven to 375°F.

Trim fennel and cut each one lengthwise into 4 pieces, leaving each attached to some of the core. Heat 1 Tbsp. of the oil in a frying pan on medium heat and sauté fennel for about 5 minutes, until golden. Season with salt and pepper. Gently stir in olives and tomatoes, then transfer to an ovenproof baking dish.

Return the frying pan to the stove on medium heat. Heat the remaining oil, then sauté garlic, shallots, thyme and bay leaf for about 5 minutes, until fragrant. Pour in wine and stock, then deglaze the pan. Bring to a boil and pour over the fennel. Cover with aluminum foil and braise in the oven for 20 minutes, until just tender. Use a slotted spoon to transfer fennel and olives to a warmed bowl.

Add coriander seeds to the remaining liquid and reduce to half on medium-high heat. Remove from the stove and let cool for 10 minutes. Purée in a blender, then strain through a fine-mesh sieve into a clean bowl. Season this sauce with lemon juice, salt and pepper.

Add parsley to the fennel and olives. Pour sauce over the fennel mixture, then toss well. Keep warm.

SNAPPER: Preheat the broiler. Lightly butter an ovenproof baking pan.

Combine shrimp, butter, basil, bread crumbs, pine nuts, garlic, salt and pepper in a bowl. Mix thoroughly.

Season fish with salt and pepper, then place in the prepared baking pan. Spread the shrimp mixture over fish, then drizzle with wine. Broil for 7 to 8 minutes, until fish is just cooked and the crust is golden brown.

TO SERVE: Place 2 pieces of fennel in each large shallow bowl, add one quarter of the sauce, then top with a fillet of red snapper. Drizzle with oil.

WINE: Try Barrique, an oak-aged blend of Pinot Gris and Auxerrois from Arrowleaf, with its full, smooth, subtle apple taste.

Shrimp and Basil-crusted Red Snapper with Olive-braised Fennel

Prosciutto-wrapped Grilled Scallops

with Sunchoke-Watercress Salad

SALAD

1 to 2 sunchokes,
peeled and sliced

6 tiny florets of broccoli

3 segments ruby grapefruit

1 cup watercress, destemmed

3 oven-dried tomato halves
or 1 fresh tomato, peeled,
seeded and slivered

1 tsp. chopped fresh chives

VINAIGRETTE

2 Tbsp. extra-virgin olive oil

1 tsp. sherry vinegar

Drop of fresh lemon juice

½ tsp. Dijon mustard

¼ tsp. chopped fresh tarragon

GARNISH (OPTIONAL)

2 tsp. olive oil

1 sunchoke, peeled
and thinly sliced

1 clove garlic, thinly sliced

SCALLOPS

1 to 2 slices prosciutto,
cut in half lengthwise

2 to 3 large fresh scallops

1 tsp. vegetable oil

SUNCHOKES are also known as Jerusalem artichokes. If you cannot find them, use asparagus. *Serves 1*

SALAD: Fill 2 bowls with ice water. Bring 2 saucepans of salted water to a boil on high heat. Add sunchokes to one saucepan and broccoli to the other. Cook until vegetables are just tender, about 3 to 4 minutes for sunchokes and 2 to 3 minutes for broccoli. Transfer each vegetable to a separate bowl of ice water and let cool. Drain and pat dry with paper towels.

Toss together sunchokes, broccoli, grapefruit, watercress, tomatoes and chives in a bowl.

VINAIGRETTE: Place all the ingredients in a bowl. Season with salt and pepper. Whisk until emulsified.

GARNISH (optional): Heat oil in a frying pan on medium-high heat. Fry sunchokes and garlic for 3 to 4 minutes, until crisp. Drain on paper towels.

SCALLOPS: Wrap a half slice of prosciutto around the sides of each scallop. Heat oil in a nonstick frying pan on medium-high heat. Sauté wrapped scallops for about 2 minutes per side, until they are just warm in the middle.

TO SERVE: Toss salad with enough vinaigrette to just moisten the vegetables. Arrange the salad in the middle of a plate. Top with the scallops and drizzle with the remaining dressing. Garnish (optional) with sunchokes and garlic.

WINE: Sip a crisp pink Pinot Gris from Alderlea or a fresh one from Burrowing Owl.

Smoked Salmon Tartare

WE MAKE THIS TARTARE with our signature beechwood-smoked wild pink salmon, which is sold at many fine food stores—but any good-quality smoked salmon will do. The dressing is in the style of ponzu, a traditional Japanese citrus and soy dipping sauce for sashimi. You can also use it as a dressing for salad. *Serves 6 to 8*

DRESSING: Combine lemon juice, vinegar, soy sauce and mirin in a bowl.

TARTARE: In a chilled glass or stainless steel bowl, very gently mix salmon with daikon, apple, green onions and dressing. Marinate in the refrigerator for 2 hours.

TO SERVE: Divide the tartare among individual Chinese ceramic soupspoons. Serve chilled.

WINE: Try the dependable sparkling Sumac Ridge Steller's Jay Brut.

DRESSING

1 Tbsp. fresh lemon juice

1 Tbsp. Japanese rice vinegar

2 Tbsp. Japanese soy sauce

1 Tbsp. mirin (page 13)

TARTARE

14 oz. cold-smoked wild pink salmon, skin removed, in 1/8-inch dice

1/3 cup finely diced daikon

1/2 small tart apple, cored, peeled and finely diced

2 green onions, finely diced

2 to 3 Tbsp. ponzu-style dressing

{ C RESTAURANT: *robert clark* }

Seared Sea Scallops with Hazelnut Butter, and Orange and Fennel Salad

Seared Sea Scallops

with Hazelnut Butter, and Orange and Fennel Salad

YOU CAN MAKE the hazelnut butter ahead of time. Use as many hazelnuts as you like, and refrigerate leftovers for up to 1 month. Try hazelnut butter on your morning toast too!

At C, we never pepper scallops because the pepper gives the impression that you are eating sand. *Serves 4*

HAZELNUT BUTTER: Preheat the oven to 350°F.

Spread hazelnuts on a cookie sheet, then bake in the oven for 10 to 15 minutes, until golden. Transfer to a clean tea towel and rub them gently to remove the skins. Let cool. Place in a food processor and grind until the mixture is the consistency of peanut butter.

SALAD: Working over a bowl, slip a small paring knife between the membrane and the flesh of each orange segment. Allow the juice and orange segments to collect in the bowl. Strain the orange juice into a bowl and save.

In another bowl, toss together orange segments, fennel, shallots and vinegar. Season with salt and pepper, then let macerate for 1 hour.

DRESSING: Place mustard, anise seed, honey, lime juice and 1 Tbsp. of the reserved orange juice in a blender. With the motor running, slowly add oil. Season with salt and pepper.

SCALLOPS: Pat scallops dry with paper towels to get rid of moisture so they will brown nicely while cooking. Heat oil in a frying pan on medium-high heat. Place scallops one at a time in the pan, making sure there is a little space between them so that they fry rather than boil. Season with salt and cook for 1 minute, until they start to turn golden brown. Turn the scallops over and cook for 30 seconds, until slightly underdone. Remove from the heat and toss the hot scallops with 1 Tbsp. of the hazelnut butter.

TO SERVE: Place three scallops in the centre of each plate. Arrange some salad on top and drizzle the dressing around the plate. Serve warm.

WINE: Complement this dish with a Pinot Gris from Tinhorn Creek or from Gray Monk's regular or Odyssey series.

HAZELNUT BUTTER
½ lb. hazelnuts

SALAD
2 oranges, peeled and white pith removed

1 bulb fennel, thinly sliced

2 shallots, thinly sliced

1 Tbsp. tarragon vinegar

DRESSING
1 tsp. Dijon mustard

½ tsp. anise seed

1 tsp. honey

1 tsp. lime juice

2 Tbsp. extra-virgin olive oil

SCALLOPS
12 large scallops, preferably diver scallops

1 Tbsp. vegetable oil

Birch Syrup-glazed Pacific Wild Salmon
with Rye Berry Salad

SALMON

4 fillets wild salmon, each 6 oz.

2 Tbsp. birch syrup or
maple syrup

1 Tbsp. vegetable oil

SALAD

2 Tbsp. unsalted butter

1 onion, finely diced

1-inch piece of fresh ginger

1 clove garlic, unpeeled

2 bay leaves

1 cup rye berries

2 cups water

1 Tbsp. tarragon vinegar

1 tsp. Dijon mustard

1 tsp. honey

1 cup cherry tomatoes,
quartered

DRESSING

4 Tbsp. finely diced double-
smoked bacon

4 shallots, finely diced

2 Tbsp. olive oil or garlic oil

1 Tbsp. sherry vinegar

THE COOKING TIME of salmon varies according to its thickness. Measure the fish at it thickest part, and cook it for 8 to 10 minutes per inch. Be very careful not to overcook the salmon. *Serves 4*

SALMON: Season salmon with salt and pepper. Pour syrup into a shallow baking dish, then arrange salmon on it, skin side up. Let fish marinate for 1 hour at room temperature. (Refrigerate the fish if you marinate it longer.)

SALAD: Melt butter in a frying pan on medium-high heat. Sauté onion, ginger, garlic and bay leaves for 10 minutes, until onions are translucent. Add rye berries and cook for 1 minute. Add water and bring to a boil, then turn down the heat to low and simmer for about 45 minutes, until rye berries are tender. Drain, then remove and discard ginger, garlic and bay leaves.

Place rye berries in a bowl and toss with vinegar, mustard and honey. Season to taste with salt and pepper. Gently stir in tomatoes.

DRESSING: Sauté bacon in a frying pan on medium-hot heat for about 5 minutes, until crisp. Drain bacon on paper towels. Turn down the heat to low. Drain off and discard all but 1 Tbsp. of the bacon fat from the frying pan. Sauté shallots for 2 to 3 minutes, until translucent. Transfer shallots to a bowl and combine with oil and vinegar. Add bacon, then season with salt and pepper.

FINISH SALMON: Preheat the oven to 375°F. Lightly grease a baking pan with oil.

Use a slotted spoon to transfer salmon to the baking pan and bake in the oven for about 5 minutes, until cooked to desired doneness.

TO SERVE: Add some dressing to the salad and toss, then arrange on individual plates. Top the salad with a piece of salmon and drizzle with some of the remaining dressing.

WINE: Match this salmon with a Pinot Noir from Kettle Valley Winery, either the Foxtrot or Hayman selections.

Baked Cornbread and Quinoa Pudding

with Roasted Tomato Coulis and Basil-Zucchini Essence

FOR A QUICK FAMILY DINNER, make this delicious meatless pudding in a large gratin dish. *Serves 4*

COULIS: Preheat the broiler. Place tomatoes in a shallow roasting pan. Broil (about 3 inches from the heat), turning occasionally, for about 10 minutes, until the skins are blackened. Remove from the oven and let cool.

Transfer tomatoes to a shallow bowl. Peel and core, discarding the skins and cores. Cut tomatoes in half and deseed them. Strain the seeds through a fine-mesh sieve; save any juice but discard the seeds.

Chop tomatoes coarsely, then place in a blender with the reserved tomato juice, shallot, salt and pepper. Blend thoroughly, then strain through a fine-mesh sieve into a clean bowl. Save the coulis at room temperature.

BASIL-ZUCCHINI ESSENCE: Fill a bowl with ice water. Bring a pot of water to a boil, then briefly blanch zucchini, spinach and basil all together until bright green. Plunge them immediately into the bowl of ice water, then drain well.

Place blanched vegetables, tofu, salt and pepper in a blender or food processor and purée until smooth. Strain through a fine-mesh sieve into a bowl, pressing gently to extract all of the juice. Save this essence at room temperature. Discard the solids.

continued overleaf >

COULIS

2 tomatoes, preferably organic

1 shallot, thinly sliced

BASIL-ZUCCHINI ESSENCE

½ green zucchini, trimmed, deseeded and roughly sliced

Handful of fresh spinach, leaves only

Bunch or large handful of fresh basil, leaves only

2 Tbsp. silken tofu

Pinch of sea salt and freshly ground black pepper

PUDDING: Preheat the oven to 375°F. Grease four 1-cup ramekins with vegetable spray.

Lightly toss together quinoa, cornbread, shallots, bell pepper, mozzarella, roasted garlic, thyme, sea salt and black pepper in a bowl.

In another bowl, combine milk, cream and eggs. Mix well, then strain through a fine-mesh sieve. Pour over the quinoa-cornbread mixture and mix lightly. Do not overmix.

Fill ramekins to the top with the pudding mixture and carefully tap them on the counter to get rid of any air bubbles. Place the ramekins in a large roasting pan and add enough hot water to reach halfway up the sides of the dishes. Bake in the oven for 20 to 25 minutes, until a toothpick inserted in the custard comes out clean and the puddings are set. Remove the ramekins from the roasting pan and let cool.

TO SERVE: Spoon tomato coulis into the centre of individual warmed plates. Dip the bottom of each ramekin in warm water. Run a knife around the edge of the pudding, then carefully unmould it into your hand. Place the pudding on the coulis. Repeat with the remaining puddings. Drizzle the essence around each plate, then garnish with a sprig of fresh basil and some freshly ground black pepper.

WINE: Perfect with a classic Riesling from Wild Goose Vineyards.

Baked Cornbread and Quinoa Pudding with Roasted Tomato Coulis and Basil-Zucchini Essence

Braised Star Anise-infused Bison Short Ribs
with Wildflower Honey and Chili Glaze

MARINADE

8 pieces star anise

2 tsp. cardamom seeds

1 Tbsp. ground coriander

4 cups soy sauce

2 heads garlic, minced

2 Tbsp. black
peppercorns, ground

2/3 cup fresh lemon juice

2 onions, finely ground
in a food processor

4 Tbsp. minced fresh ginger

3/4 cup demerara sugar or
organic cane sugar

1/3 cup safflower oil

2 Tbsp. minced lemon grass

1 3/4 cups water

2 Tbsp. sambal oelek
or to taste

SHORT RIBS

5 lbs. bison short ribs or
organic beef ribs

1/2 cup wild blackberry honey
or other wildflower honey

Sambal oelek to taste

Vegetable spray to grease pan

THE MARINADE in this recipe will keep for up to 6 months in the refrigerator. You can also use it to marinate salmon or as a stir-fry sauce for chicken or beef. To save time, you can cook the short ribs a day ahead. Once they are cooked, strain the cooking liquid through a fine-mesh sieve into a clean bowl. Refrigerate the meat and the cooking liquid in separate containers. Gently warm the ribs with the glaze before serving.

Serve these short ribs with garlic mashed potatoes and a combination of steamed green and yellow beans. *Serves 4*

MARINADE: Place star anise and cardamom seeds in a small dry frying pan on medium heat. Shake the pan gently and toast for 3 to 4 minutes, until the spices smell fragrant.

Combine all the ingredients in a stainless steel saucepan on medium heat. Bring to a boil, then turn down the heat to low and simmer for 20 minutes. Remove from the heat and let cool to room temperature, then store in a tightly sealed glass container and refrigerate until needed.

SHORT RIBS: Preheat the oven to 375°F. Wash short ribs and pat them dry with paper towels. Place them in a roasting pan, meat side down.

Combine 2 cups of the marinade with 2 cups of water and pour over short ribs. Make sure that ribs are totally immersed. If they are not, add more marinade and water in equal amounts. Place the pan on medium-high heat and bring the marinade to a boil. Cover the pan with aluminum foil, shiny side in, then bake in the oven for 45 minutes. Check the cooking liquid. If it is boiling hard, turn down the oven temperature until the cooking liquid bubbles gently. Cook for another 75 to 105 minutes, until meat is tender and about to fall off the bones. Remove the pan from the oven and let cool slightly. Leave the oven on if you plan to continue with the recipe at this point.

Use a slotted spoon to transfer short ribs to a stainless steel bowl. Cover the ribs with aluminum foil or plastic wrap to keep them warm.

Skim off and discard the fat from the cooking liquid. Strain the cooking liquid through a fine-mesh sieve into a clean saucepan and let sit for 10 minutes. Skim off and discard fat again. Bring the cooking liquid to a boil on medium-high heat, then cook for about 15 minutes, until reduced to one quarter. (If the sauce becomes too salty before it is fully reduced, combine 1 to 2 tsp. of corn-starch with ¼ cup cold water in a small cup and stir the mixture into the sauce to bind it, then cook until it has the consistency of a glaze.) Add honey and season with sambal oelek. Remove from heat but keep the glaze warm.

Line a roasting pan with aluminum foil, grease with vegetable spray and arrange short ribs in it. Brush with plenty of glaze and reheat in the oven for 10 minutes, until heated through.

TO SERVE: Divide the ribs among warmed dinner plates and drizzle with extra glaze.

WINE: Partner with a glass of Sandhill Syrah, part of the small lots program, from Phantom Creek Vineyard.

Organic Field Berry and Wild Peppermint Preserve

10 sprigs fresh peppermint
(Lady Rosenthal, if available)

1 cup assorted fresh
organic berries

1 cup wildflower honey

1 orange, zest and juice of

2 tsp. fresh spearmint leaves,
in chiffonade

USE WHATEVER BERRIES are in season for the preserve. We particularly like blackberries, blackcap raspberries and currants. The preserve will keep refrigerated for up to 5 days. *Serves 6*

Use a meat pounder or mallet to lightly hit peppermint stems to release their flavour. Place peppermint, berries, honey and orange zest and juice in a saucepan. Use a potato masher to gently crush the mixture but be careful not to pulverize it. Let stand at room temperature for 2 to 3 hours.

Place the saucepan on medium heat and slowly bring the berry mixture to a simmer, stirring occasionally. Remove from the heat and let cool. Remove and discard peppermint sprigs, then cover the saucepan with a lid and refrigerate the preserve overnight.

Remove the preserve from the refrigerator and stir. Add additional honey, if needed. Stir in spearmint.

TO SERVE: Spoon preserves over vanilla ice cream or sliced peaches or a slice of pound cake.

WINE: Pair with a fruit wine, such as apricot or cassis or even the handpicked frozen Fuji apples made into icewine, from Elephant Island Orchard Winery in Naramata.

Roasted Chestnut Soup

INSTEAD OF ROASTING your own chestnuts, you may purchase roasted and peeled chestnuts packed in jars or bags. These are available from specialty food stores, as is canned chestnut purée. I recommend the 15½-oz. can of Faugier brand chestnut purée, but be sure that you do not pick up the kind that is sweetened. *Serves 6*

1 lb. chestnuts, about 28 to 30
3 Tbsp. butter
½ clove garlic
1 shallot, minced
¼ cup Noilly Prat or other dry white vermouth
4 cups vegetable stock
1 cup whipping cream
½ lemon, juice of

Preheat the oven to 350°F. Use a sharp knife to score the flat side of each chestnut with an "x." Place the chestnuts in a roasting pan and roast in the oven for about 15 minutes, until the cut shells curl. Remove from the oven and let cool. Peel off the outer shell and the inner skin.

Heat 1 Tbsp. of the butter in a saucepan on medium heat. Sauté garlic and shallot for about 5 minutes, until translucent. Add vermouth and deglaze the pan. Continue to cook for 1 to 2 minutes, until reduced to half. Add chestnuts and stock, then bring to a simmer on medium heat and cook for 10 minutes, until chestnuts are tender. Stir in cream and simmer for 5 minutes, then remove from the heat and let cool for 10 minutes.

Purée in a blender or food processor until creamy and smooth. Transfer to a clean saucepan.

TO SERVE: Warm soup gently on low heat. Just before serving, stir in the remaining butter and lemon juice. Season with salt and pepper. Ladle into soup bowls.

WINE: Try Garry Oaks Blanc de Noir (Pinot Noir), made from Saltspring Island grapes, instead of the more traditional nutty oloroso sherry.

Grilled Ahi Tuna with Creamy Lentils
and Balsamic-Soy Sauce

LENTILS

6 slices bacon, in ¼-inch cubes

4 stalks asparagus, trimmed,
in ¼-inch rounds

1½ cups cooked Puy lentils

¼ cup whipping cream

Splash of sherry vinegar

SAUCE

½ cup unsalted butter

1 Tbsp. chopped fresh ginger

Pinch of chili flakes

1 Tbsp. tomato paste

¼ cup soy sauce

¼ cup balsamic vinegar

TUNA

2 fillets Ahi tuna, each 5 oz.

½ tsp. vegetable oil

THE BALSAMIC-SOY SAUCE is a good complement to other grilled fishes and meats. *Serves 2*

LENTILS: Sauté bacon in a frying pan on medium heat for about 15 minutes, until crisp. Drain off and discard the excess fat but keep the pan. Add asparagus and lentils, then add cream and cook gently for about 10 minutes, until all the cream is absorbed. Stir in vinegar. Keep warm.

SAUCE: Place butter, ginger, chili flakes and tomato paste in a frying pan on medium heat. Cook until butter melts, then whisk in soy sauce and vinegar. Strain through a fine-mesh sieve. Keep warm.

TUNA: Season tuna on both sides with salt and pepper. Rub a heavy frying pan or a grill pan with oil, then place on high heat. When hot, sear tuna for 2 minutes per side, until medium-rare.

TO SERVE: Place lentil mixture in the centre of each plate and top with tuna. Drizzle sauce around the edge of the plates.

WINE: This robust dish stands up to a red Merlot, such as the plummy Stag's Hollow.

{ CIN CIN RISTORANTE: *romy prasad* }

Grilled Ahi Tuna with Creamy Lentils and Balsamic-Soy Sauce

Fresh Berry Compote

SE ANY COMBINATION of fresh seasonal berries. If fresh berries are not available, you can use frozen ones or a mix of fresh and frozen. Cook frozen berries for about 2 minutes before adding fresh ones. *Serves 4*

SIMPLE SYRUP: Combine sugar and water in a small saucepan on medium heat. Bring to a boil, then cook for 1 minute, until sugar is dissolved. Let cool, then pour into an airtight container. Will keep in the refrigerator for up to 2 weeks.

COMPOTE: Combine ¼ cup of the simple syrup with orange juice in a saucepan on medium-low heat. Bring to a simmer, then add blackberries, blueberries and strawberries. Cook for 4 to 6 minutes, until soft.

TO SERVE: Ladle cooked berries and juice into individual bowls. Place a scoop of vanilla ice cream on top of the hot berries and garnish with a sprig of mint.

WINE: The Quails' Gate Optima Totally Botrytis Affected has complementary Muscat aromas and honeyed apricot flavours.

SIMPLE SYRUP

1 cup sugar

1 cup water

COMPOTE

¾ cup fresh orange juice

½ cup blackberries

½ cup blueberries

½ cup strawberries

4 scoops vanilla ice cream

4 sprigs fresh mint
for garnish

Fraser Valley Quail Salad

with Goat Cheese and Caramel Poached Pears

SECKEL PEARS are ideal for this recipe, but Bosc or Bartlett will work well too. If you cannot find small pears, simply quarter or slice larger ones.

As an alternative to aged balsamic vinegar, combine 1 cup balsamic vinegar and 1 Tbsp. brown sugar in a small saucepan on medium heat and cook for about 10 minutes, until reduced to about ⅓ cup. Use 1 Tbsp. of this reduction in the quail salad. *Serves 6*

PEARS: Preheat the oven to 425°F. Line a cookie sheet with parchment paper. Place pears, cut side down, on the cookie sheet. Brush with butter, then sprinkle with sugar. Bake in the oven for about 10 minutes, until just tender and golden. For a deeper golden appearance, turn up the oven to broil, then broil for 5 minutes.

MUSHROOMS: Heat oil in a saucepan on medium-high heat. Sauté mushrooms for about 10 minutes, until browned and any juices have been reabsorbed. Season with salt and pepper and herbs. Keep warm.

QUAIL: Preheat the oven to 400°F. Season quail with salt and pepper.

Heat 1 Tbsp. of the oil in an ovenproof frying pan on medium-high heat. Sear quail legs on one side for 3 minutes, until browned, then turn over and sear for 3 minutes. Add breasts, skin side down, and sear for 3 to 4 minutes, until browned, then turn over. Place the pan in the oven and roast for about 5 minutes, until cooked to medium. (The breast meat should remain rosy in the centre; the quail is cooked when it gives when pressed lightly with a finger.) Transfer quail to a warmed plate. Keep the roasting pan and lower the oven heat to 350°F.

To make the dressing, place the roasting pan on the stove on medium-high heat and add stock to deglaze. Stir in sherry and balsamic vinegars, and the remaining oil. Remove from the heat.

CROUTONS: Arrange baguette slices on a cookie sheet and place a piece of goat cheese on top of each. Bake in the oven for 5 minutes, until cheese is lightly melted. *continued overleaf >*

PEARS
3 small pears, peeled, cored and halved

1 Tbsp. butter, melted

1 Tbsp. sugar

MUSHROOMS
1 Tbsp. olive oil

4 oz. mixed fresh mushrooms (cremini, shiitake, portobello), destemmed

1 Tbsp. chopped mixed fresh herbs (parsley, thyme, tarragon, chives)

QUAIL
6 boneless quail, each 5 to 6 oz., use breast halves and legs only

3 Tbsp. olive oil

¼ cup chicken stock

2 Tbsp. sherry vinegar

1 Tbsp. 5- or 10-year-old balsamic vinegar

CROUTONS
6 slices French baguette, toasted lightly

6 Tbsp. soft goat cheese, in 6 small pieces

TO SERVE: Place a spoonful of mushrooms in the centre of each plate. Prop 2 quail legs and 2 breast halves against the mushrooms on each serving, then garnish with a caramelized pear half and a goat cheese crouton. Drizzle dressing over each plate.

WINE: A classy Pinot Noir is perfect here—try Quails' Gate Family Estate, aged in new French barriques.

Seared Albacore Tuna

with Ragout of Peas and Syrah Sauce

FISH FUMET is a fish stock. You may make it yourself or buy it at specialty food stores. *Serves 6*

RAGOUT: Sauté bacon in a frying pan on medium-high heat for 5 minutes, until golden. Drain off and discard the excess fat, then add peas and sauté for 3 minutes, until just tender. Keep warm, uncovered, so peas retain their bright colour.

BOUQUET GARNI: Place herbs on a piece of cheesecloth, gather up the four corners and tie closed with kitchen string.

SAUCE: Place bouquet garni, wine, shallots and orange juice in a saucepan on medium-high heat. Cook for about 5 minutes, until sauce is reduced to ½ cup. Add fish fumet and cook for about 5 minutes, until reduced to ½ cup. Remove and discard bouquet garni. Whisk in butter, then add orange segments, black and green olives, and tomatoes. Stir to combine, then remove from the heat and set aside in a warm place.

TUNA: Rub tuna on both sides with oil, then season with salt and pepper. Heat a nonreactive, nonstick frying pan on medium-high heat. Place tuna, rosemary and scallions in the pan and sear tuna for 2 minutes per side, until medium-rare. The top ⅛ inch of the tuna will be cooked on each side, and the flesh in between will be red.

TO SERVE: Place a spoonful of pea ragout in the middle of each plate. Top with a medallion of tuna, a sprig of rosemary and a scallion. Drizzle sauce over each plate.

WINE: Burrowing Owl Syrah expresses the varietal well and can even match tuna.

RAGOUT

3 slices double-smoked
bacon, in small dice

3 cups shelled
fresh English spring peas

BOUQUET GARNI

4 stems fresh parsley

1 sprig fresh thyme

1 bay leaf

2 ribs celery,
each 2 inches long

SAUCE

1 cup Syrah or other
full-bodied red wine

2 shallots, finely chopped

1 orange, juice of

¼ cup fish fumet

¼ cup cold butter, cubed

1 orange, peeled and segmented

6 black olives, pitted

6 green olives, pitted

6 cherry tomatoes or 2 tomatoes,
peeled and chopped

TUNA

6 medallions of sashimi-grade
albacore tuna, each 6 to 8 oz.

1 Tbsp. olive oil

6 small sprigs rosemary

6 scallions

Okanagan Apple Tarte Tatin
with Maple Syrup Ice Cream

ICE CREAM
1 cup milk

1 cup whipping cream

4 egg yolks

2/3 cup maple syrup

TART
1 lb. puff pastry

4 Tbsp. butter

3½ oz. sugar

4 Gala or Golden Delicious apples, peeled, cored and quartered

½ vanilla bean

1 Tbsp. + 2 tsp. raisins soaked in 1 Tbsp. + 2 tsp. rum

1 egg, beaten

Icing sugar for dusting

THIS IS A DESSERT of contrasts: hot and cold, crunchy and soft. The maple syrup ice cream melts to form a delicious sauce over the tart. *Serves 6*

ICE CREAM: Combine milk and cream in a saucepan on medium heat. Cook until scalded.

Whisk together egg yolks and maple syrup in a stainless steel bowl. Slowly add the warm milk mixture, whisking constantly. Place the bowl over a saucepan of simmering but not boiling water on lowest heat. Cook for about 5 minutes, until the custard coats the back of a spoon. Do not allow the mixture to boil. Remove from the heat and let cool, stirring occasionally.

Cover the bowl of custard with plastic wrap and refrigerate until cold. Process in an ice-cream maker according to the manufacturer's instructions.

TART: Preheat the oven to 375°F. Grease 6 ovenproof ramekins, each 2/3 to 3/4 cup.

Roll out pastry on a lightly floured work surface to a thickness of 1/8 inch. Cut 6 rounds, each slightly larger than the diameter of the ramekins. Place a pastry round on a plate, cover with waxed paper, then add another pastry round and another piece of waxed paper. Repeat process with the remaining rounds. Cover the plate with waxed paper, then place the stack in the refrigerator to chill.

Melt butter on medium heat in a frying pan large enough to hold the apples. Add sugar and cook for about 5 minutes, until medium caramel in colour. Add apples and vanilla bean, then cook for 8 to 10 minutes, until apples are just tender. Gently stir in raisins and rum. Remove vanilla bean. (Rinsed, dried and wrapped in plastic wrap, it can be refrigerated and reused.)

Use a slotted spoon to transfer apples and raisins to the buttered ramekins. Drizzle the cooking syrup over the apples.

Fill a small bowl with water. Dip a finger in the water and run it around the inside edge of each ramekin. Cover each ramekin with a pastry disk, making sure to press the edges of the pastry to the moistened rim of the ramekin to form a tight seal. Brush the pastry with beaten egg.

Place the ramekins in a large roasting pan and add enough hot water to reach halfway up the sides of the dishes. Bake in the oven for 35 to 40 minutes, until pastry is golden brown.

TO SERVE: Dip the bottom of each ramekin in warm water and run a knife around the edge of the pastry. Place a plate over the top of each ramekin, then invert both the plate and the ramekin. Remove the ramekin. The caramel will flow over the fruit.

Place a spoonful of icing sugar in a sieve and sift a little over each tart. Top with a scoop of maple syrup ice cream.

WINE: Riesling icewines from Jackson-Triggs, always a treat, are an especially brilliant accompaniment to apple desserts.

Lamb Shanks Braised with Chardonnay and Fennel

SPICE SACHET

1 orange, zest only

2 Tbsp. fennel seeds

1 tsp. mustard seeds

1 Tbsp. black peppercorns

2 bay leaves

6 sprigs fresh thyme

LAMB

6 to 8 cups chicken stock

6 lamb shanks, trimmed
and wiped clean

Kosher salt and freshly
ground black pepper

4 Tbsp. canola oil

1 carrot, peeled, in large dice

1 rib celery, in large dice

2 onions, in large dice

2 bulbs fennel, hard core
removed, in large dice

4 cloves garlic, crushed

5 ½-oz. can tomato paste

26-oz. bottle Chardonnay

ORANGE AND FENNEL go well together. To obtain the orange zest for the spice sachet, use a potato peeler to carefully remove only the orange-coloured part of the orange peel. Use these strips of peel in the sachet.

To save time, you can cook the lamb shanks a day ahead. Serve them with mashed potatoes or white beans. *Serves 6*

SPICE SACHET: Place all the ingredients on a large piece of cheesecloth, gather up the four corners and tie closed with kitchen string.

LAMB: Preheat the oven to 325°F.

Place stock in a saucepan on medium-high heat and bring to a boil. Turn down the heat and keep warm.

Season lamb with kosher salt and black pepper. Heat 2 Tbsp. of the oil in a frying pan on high heat. Sear lamb, in batches, for 5 minutes each, until browned on all sides. Transfer to an ovenproof pot and save the frying pan.

Add the remaining oil to the frying pan on medium heat. Sauté carrot, celery, onions, fennel and garlic for 8 to 10 minutes, until golden. Stir in tomato paste and wine, then bring to a boil. Pour over lamb. Add enough hot stock to completely cover lamb and vegetables. Add the spice sachet, then cover the pot with a lid or aluminum foil. Braise in the oven for 3 to 4 hours, until lamb is fork-tender and nearly falls off the bone. Remove from the oven.

Discard the spice sachet. Transfer lamb to a platter and keep warm. Skim off and discard the fat from the cooking liquid, then strain it through a fine-mesh sieve into a clean saucepan. Discard the vegetables. If you prefer a thicker sauce, bring the cooking liquid to a boil on medium-high heat and cook until reduced to the desired consistency. (Can be made up to this point a day ahead; refrigerate lamb and sauce separately.)

TO SERVE: Place the lamb in the sauce and reheat gently on medium heat. Arrange lamb and sauce on a serving platter or on individual plates.

WINE: Sweet smoky oaked Mission Hill Shiraz is sublime.

Lamb Shanks Braised with Chardonnay and Fennel

Plum Johnnycake Cobblers

SERVE THESE COBBLERS warm with a scoop of vanilla ice cream or a dollop of whipped cream. *Serves 6*

SPICE SACHET: Place all the ingredients on a piece of cheesecloth, gather up the four corners and tie closed with kitchen string.

BASE: Place butter and sugar in a saucepan on medium heat. Cook while stirring for about 5 minutes, until butter is melted and sugar is dissolved. Add plums, stir to coat with the syrup and cook for 3 to 4 minutes, until they release some of their juice. Add the spice sachet and wine, then simmer on medium heat, stirring occasionally, for about 10 minutes, until most of the liquid evaporates.

TOPPING: Place flour, cornmeal, sugar, baking powder, baking soda, kosher salt, ground ginger and fresh ginger in a blender or food processor. Pulse to mix. Add butter, then pulse until the mixture has the texture of coarse meal.

Transfer to a bowl. Slowly add cream, mixing gently with a fork, to make a soft, moist dough that forms curds.

TO ASSEMBLE: Preheat the oven to 425°F. Grease six ¾-cup ramekins.

Divide the plum mixture among the ramekins, then cover with the biscuit topping. Bake in the oven for 12 to 15 minutes, until topping is golden brown.

TO SERVE: Place each ramekin on a napkin-lined plate.

WINE: Tinhorn Creek Kerner Late Harvest has appropriate sweet spicy tropical fruit, or Gehringer Brothers Cabernet Franc Icewine is reminiscent of a very fruity port.

SPICE SACHET

1 star anise

2 pieces of fresh ginger, each the size of a quarter

3 cardamom pods

BASE

3 Tbsp. butter

¼ cup sugar

4 cups sliced damson or prune plums

½ cup port or other fruity red wine

TOPPING

¾ cup all-purpose flour

¼ cup cornmeal

2 Tbsp. sugar

1½ tsp. baking powder

¼ tsp. baking soda

½ tsp. kosher salt

½ tsp. ground ginger

½ tsp. finely minced fresh ginger

2 Tbsp. cold butter, cubed

½ cup whipping cream

Golden Pineapple and Mango Carpaccio
with Mint and Lemon Sorbet

SORBET
½ cup sugar

½ cup water

⅔ cup milk

⅔ cup fresh lemon juice

2 lemons, grated zest of

CARPACCIO
1 ripe Hawaiian pineapple,
peeled, all brown
spots removed

1 ripe mango, peeled

40 mint leaves

1 cup sugar

4 vanilla beans, split lengthwise

1 tsp. icing sugar

FOR A TART TWIST, use kalamansi limes in place of the lemons. These limes, which taste like a cross between a lemon and a mandarin orange, are sold in Asian food stores. *Serves 8*

SORBET: Make syrup by placing sugar and water in a saucepan on medium-high heat. Bring to a boil, then turn down the heat to low and simmer until sugar is dissolved. Remove from the heat and let cool.

Combine syrup, milk, lemon juice and zest in a bowl, mixing well. Transfer to an ice-cream maker and process according to the manufacturer's instructions. Freeze for up to 2 days.

CARPACCIO: Preheat the oven to 280°F. Line a cookie sheet with parchment paper.

Use a mandoline to cut 8 thin horizontal slices from the top of the pineapple, then remove and discard the core from each. Place slices on the prepared cookie sheet and bake in the oven for about 35 minutes, until golden and crispy. Let cool. Store in an airtight container until you are ready to assemble the dessert.

While pineapple slices are baking, use the mandoline to slice the remaining pineapple lengthwise into paper-thin strips. When you reach the core, give the pineapple a quarter of a turn and continue to slice paper-thin strips. Slice strips from the remaining two sides, then discard the core. Place pineapple slices on a plate.

Use the mandoline to slice mango lengthwise into paper-thin strips. Discard the pit. Place mango slices on a plate.

Place mint leaves and sugar in a blender and pulse until thoroughly combined and dark green in colour.

Scrape off seeds from vanilla pod, add to mint mixture and pulse until well mixed. (Save the vanilla bean husks for another use.)

TO SERVE: Arrange the uncooked pineapple and mango slices on individual plates. Sprinkle with the mint mixture. Garnish with a scoop of sorbet and a slice of baked pineapple. Dust with icing sugar sifted through a sieve.

WINE: The honey and pineapple flavours in the Black Hills Sequentia late harvest (of mainly Sauvignon Blanc with a dash of Semillon) are perfect here.

{ DIVA AT THE MET/SENSES BAKERY: *thomas haas* }

Golden Pineapple and Mango Carpaccio with Mint and Lemon Sorbet

Cocoa and Red Wine–braised Beef Short Ribs with Chorizo-spiced Black Bean Cakes and Jicama Slaw

Cocoa and Red Wine-braised Beef Short Ribs

with Chorizo-spiced Black Bean Cakes and Jicama Slaw

THIS DISH is perfect ski cabin fare because you can make it at home then reheat it. To save time and improve the flavour for a rustic meal at home, cook the beans and the short ribs a day ahead.

Epazote is a pungent, wild herb that is also an anti-flatulent. Look for it at Mexican or Asian specialty stores. *Serves 6*

SLAW: Toss together all the ingredients in a bowl. Cover and refrigerate for 2 to 3 hours, tossing occasionally.

SPICE SACHET: Place all the ingredients on a piece of cheesecloth, gather up the four corners and tie closed with kitchen string.

SHORT RIBS: Preheat the oven to 300°F (unless cooking on the stove top). Wipe short ribs with paper towels and season with salt and pepper.

Heat oil in a deep-sided, ovenproof saucepan on medium-high heat. Brown ribs, a few at a time, on all sides. Do not crowd the pan or the meat will steam and not brown. Transfer ribs to a plate and set aside. Add onion, carrot, celery and tomatoes to the saucepan. Cook until onion softens a bit and vegetables are slightly caramelized. Return ribs to the saucepan and add wine. Bring to a boil, then turn down the heat to low so that the mixture simmers.

Add spice sachet. Cut a piece of parchment paper the same diameter as the saucepan and place it on top of the contents. Cover with a lid, then braise in the oven for about 1½ hours (or simmer on low heat on top of the stove for about the same length of time), until meat is fork-tender. After the first 45 minutes, check meat at 10-minute intervals for doneness.

When meat is done, remove and discard spice sachet. Use tongs to transfer the ribs to a plate. Pass the braising liquid through a food mill or sieve. (Can be made up to this point a day ahead; refrigerate ribs and braising liquid separately.) *continued overleaf >*

SLAW

4 oz. jicama, julienned

½ cup fresh cilantro leaves

4 radishes, preferably rainbow, julienned

2 Tbsp. fresh lime juice

6 Tbsp. extra-virgin olive oil

Splash of tequila

Sea salt and freshly ground black pepper

SPICE SACHET

6 sprigs fresh basil

3 sprigs fresh rosemary

6 sprigs fresh tarragon

1 cinnamon stick

SHORT RIBS

2¼ lbs. beef short ribs, in 3-inch pieces

¼ cup canola oil

1 onion, chopped

1 carrot, chopped

3 ribs celery, chopped

4 very ripe tomatoes or a 14 oz.-can of plum tomatoes, undrained but chopped

25.4-oz. bottle Merlot or Sangiovese

2/3 oz. bittersweet chocolate (preferably Denman Island), chopped

½ tsp. ground coffee

BLACK BEAN CAKES

1 cup black beans, soaked
in water overnight

¼ cup + 1 Tbsp. duck fat
or vegetable oil

4 oz. chorizo, removed from
casing and chopped

1 onion, chopped

¼ bulb fennel, chopped

4 cloves garlic, crushed

¼ tsp. epazote (optional)

½ tsp. ground cumin

½ tsp. ground coriander

2 bay leaves

¼ cup molasses

Cornmeal for dusting

Sprigs of cilantro for garnish

BLACK BEAN CAKES: While the ribs are cooking, drain soaked beans and discard the water. Place beans in a saucepan and add enough fresh water to just cover them. Cook on medium-low heat for about 1 hour, until tender. Drain and discard cooking liquid.

Heat ¼ cup of the fat in a saucepan on medium-high heat. Add chorizo, onion, fennel, garlic, epazote (optional), ground cumin, ground coriander and bay leaves, then cook for 10 minutes, until onion is tender. Stir in beans and molasses (and more fat if beans look dry). Season with salt and pepper, then purée in a blender, food processor or food mill. Transfer to a clean bowl and let cool. Refrigerate until you are ready to finish cooking them. (Can be made up to this point a day ahead.)

FINISH SHORT RIBS: Remove and discard obvious fat from ribs. Remove and discard fat that has hardened on top of the braising liquid. Cook braising liquid in a saucepan on medium heat until thick enough to coat a spoon, then whisk in chocolate and coffee. Add ribs, then season with salt and pepper. Heat ribs through.

FINISH BEAN CAKES: Form the bean mixture into 6 cakes, 3 inches in diameter and 1½ inches thick. Dust with cornmeal.

Heat the remaining fat in a nonstick frying pan on medium-high heat. Fry bean cakes until heated through.

TO SERVE: Place a black bean cake on each warmed plate. Lean a short rib up against the cake and spoon a little sauce over it. Add a mound of slaw to the side and garnish with a sprig of cilantro.

WINE: Pair with Sumac Ridge berry-flavoured Meritage from Black Sage Vineyard or their super blend Pinnacle, aged two years in small oak casks.

Rhubarb Study

(Rhubarb Streusel Cake with Jasmine-infused Strawberry Compote and Fruit Leather)

YOU CAN MAKE the fruit leather 1 to 2 days ahead, then place the pieces between layers of waxed paper and store in a tightly sealed container. Use to garnish this dessert, or serve on its own in children's lunch boxes or as an afternoon snack.

Serve this dessert with a small scoop of good-quality vanilla ice cream, or present it without the ice cream as part of a brunch menu. *Serves 12*

FRUIT LEATHER: Preheat the oven to 200°F. Line 2 cookie sheets with parchment paper.

Place rhubarb, sugar and salt in a saucepan on medium heat and cook for 15 minutes, until rhubarb is soft. Remove from the heat and stir in strawberries. Purée in a blender or food processor.

Spread the fruit mixture ⅛-inch thick over the parchment paper. Bake in the oven for about 3 hours, until completely dry. Let cool. Cut the fruit leather into desired shapes.

STREUSEL TOPPING: Combine all of the ingredients in an electric mixer with a paddle attachment. Mix until crumbly. Transfer to a small bowl and set aside. Clean the mixing bowl.

CAKE: Preheat the oven to 325°F. Grease a 9 × 13-inch baking pan.

Sift together cake flour, all-purpose flour, baking soda and salt into a small bowl.

Cream together butter and sugar in the electric mixer for about 3 minutes on medium-high speed, until light and fluffy. Add eggs, one at a time, beating well after each addition. Stir in vanilla and buttermilk. Stir in the dry mixture, then fold in rhubarb.

Pour the batter into the prepared baking pan and sprinkle with streusel topping. Bake in the oven for 40 to 45 minutes, until a skewer inserted into the centre comes out clean. Let cake cool in the pan on a wire rack. *continued overleaf >*

FRUIT LEATHER

1 lb. rhubarb, in 1-inch pieces

1½ to 2 cups sugar or to taste

Pinch of salt

½ lb. fresh strawberries

STREUSEL TOPPING

½ cup brown sugar

1 tsp. ground cinnamon

½ cup butter

1 cup less 1 Tbsp. all-purpose flour

1 cup rolled oats

CAKE

1 cup cake flour

1½ cups all-purpose flour

1 tsp. baking soda

1 tsp. salt

½ cup unsalted butter

1½ cups brown sugar

2 eggs

1 tsp. vanilla extract

1 cup buttermilk

3 cups finely chopped rhubarb

Sprigs of fresh mint for garnish

COMPOTE

2 Tbsp. jasmine tea leaves

½ cup boiling water

1 cup freshly squeezed
orange juice

1½ lbs. rhubarb, chopped
into 1-inch lengths

1½ cups sugar

Pinch of ground cinnamon

1½ lbs. fresh strawberries,
hulled and quartered

COMPOTE: Place tea leaves and water in a bowl. Let infuse for 15 minutes. Strain into a clean saucepan and discard the leaves.

To the tea water, add orange juice, rhubarb, sugar and cinnamon. Simmer on medium-low heat for 15 minutes, until rhubarb is tender. Remove from the heat. Add strawberries and let cool.

TO SERVE: Cut the warm cake into 3-inch squares. Cut each square in half diagonally to make two triangles. Place 2 triangles at an angle to each other on each plate. Spoon some compote around the cake and garnish with a piece of fruit leather and a sprig of mint.

WINE: Serve with Paradise Ranch Merlot Late Harvest or Domaine de Chaberton's apricot and orange Optima Dessert wine, packaged in an exquisite cobalt blue bottle.

Lancashire Hot Pot

THIS STEW originated in Lancashire and is named for the deep pottery vessel in which it was cooked. Families would fill the dish with mutton and lamb neck (truly the tastiest part of the animal), then take it to the village baker, who put the hot pots into the community bread oven to cook. Today, the traditional mutton and lamb neck have been largely replaced with lamb loin or leftover cuts of leg or shoulder. Try making the Irish version, which uses apples and replaces the stock with a stout, such as Guinness. *Serves 4*

3 Tbsp. vegetable oil

1 lb. (about 2 large) onions, thinly sliced

1¼ to 1½ lbs. lamb loin or lamb neck, in 1-inch cubes

2 lamb kidneys (optional), each 3 oz., in ½-inch cubes

1 lb. potatoes, thinly sliced

1 cup lamb stock or chicken stock

2 Tbsp. butter, melted

Preheat the oven to 350°F. Grease a 6-cup ovenproof baking dish and season it with salt and pepper.

Heat oil in a frying pan on medium heat. Sauté onions, stirring occasionally, for 50 to 60 minutes, until caramelized. (If necessary to prevent onions from burning, reduce heat to low.) Remove from the heat.

Cover the bottom of the prepared ovenproof dish with half of the lamb. Arrange one third of the potatoes on top of the lamb. Pour half of the stock over this, then add a layer of half of the onions. Add a layer of the remaining lamb followed by another third of the potatoes. Pour the rest of the stock over this, then layer on the remaining onions. Finish with the last third of the potatoes, then brush with butter. Cover with a lid, then bake in the oven for 2 hours.

TO SERVE: Place the hot pot on the table. Use a large spoon to serve individual portions.

WINE: Tinhorn Creek has blackberry fruit and oak balance in both its softer Merlot and its more tannic, higher-acidity, peppery Cabernet Franc.

Bread and Butter Pudding

2 cups milk or
whipping cream

3 eggs

¼ cup sugar

3 to 4 Tbsp. unsalted butter

4 to 6 slices good-quality
white bread or croissants

½ cup sultanas or raisins

1 orange, zest of

BREAD PUDDING is a tasty way to use leftover bread or croissants. It is also a homey dessert that is comfort food to many. You can dress up this pudding with a caramel sauce and a small scoop of vanilla ice cream. *Serves 6*

Preheat the oven to 300°F. Grease a 5-cup ovenproof baking dish or soufflé pan.

Whisk together milk, eggs and sugar in a bowl. Set the custard aside.

Spread butter on one side of each slice of bread. Cover the bottom of the baking dish with one third of the bread. Sprinkle half of the sultanas on top, followed by the orange zest. Arrange a third of the bread over the orange zest, then sprinkle with the remaining sultanas. Finish with the last third of the bread.

Slowly pour the custard into the baking dish. Set the dish in a large roasting pan and add enough hot water to reach halfway up the sides of the dish. Bake in the oven for about 25 minutes, until custard sets. Remove from the oven, then take out the baking dish from the roasting pan.

TO SERVE: Spoon warm bread pudding onto individual plates.

WINE: Domaine de Chaberton Ortega Botrytis Affected has melony exotic ripe fruits to complement this pudding.

Spicy Japanese Eggplant with Crispy Calamari

SHISO is Japanese basil. Kewpie mayonnaise is sold in Japanese specialty stores.

If you do not have a deep fryer, heat ¼-inch of oil (about ½ cup) in a deep, straight-sided frying pan and fry the squid in small batches. You can prepare the calamari while the eggplant is cooking. *Serves 4*

EGGPLANT: Heat 3 Tbsp. of the oil in a frying pan on medium-high heat until hot but not smoking. Sauté eggplant until golden, stirring or shaking the pan to brown all sides. (You will need to add more oil as the eggplant cooks, but not so much that it gets too greasy.) Cook until eggplant is tender, about 7 minutes. Remove from the heat.

CALAMARI: Preheat the oil in a deep fryer to 350°F.

Rinse squid under cold water, then drain and pat dry. Place in a bowl, cover and refrigerate until needed.

Place flour in large bowl and season with salt, pepper and paprika. Dredge squid in flour, then place in a sieve over a small bowl. Shake the sieve gently so the excess flour falls into the bowl. Discard the excess flour.

Deep-fry squid for 1 to 2 minutes, until golden. Be careful not to overcook squid or it will become rubbery. Use a slotted spoon to remove the squid and drain on paper towels.

FINISH EGGPLANT: Toss eggplant with cayenne, then add shiso and toss again. Add soy sauce and deglaze the pan, tossing eggplant to glaze it. Remove from the heat immediately.

TO SERVE: Arrange a row of stacked eggplant in the middle of each plate, then top with calamari. Squeeze a little Kewpie mayonnaise into the centre of the top squid ring, then drizzle sweet chili sauce around each plate.

WINE: A good match for the rose petals and lychee nut statement of Red Rooster Gewurztraminer.

EGGPLANT

4 to 8 Tbsp. sesame oil

3 Japanese eggplants, in 3 × ¼-inch batons (sticks)

Pinch of cayenne pepper

6 leaves shiso, in chiffonade

2 Tbsp. soy sauce

CALAMARI

3½ to 4 cups peanut or vegetable oil for frying

1 lb. squid tubes, cleaned, in ½-inch rounds

1½ cups all-purpose flour

Pinch of smoked paprika "picante" or Hungarian hot paprika

3 Tbsp. Kewpie or regular mayonnaise

3 Tbsp. Thai sweet chili sauce

Pan-roasted Ling Cod with Clam Vinaigrette

CLAM VINAIGRETTE

2 lbs. fresh clams, washed
and drained

6 Tbsp. Noilly Prat or other
dry white vermouth

1 Yukon Gold potato, in small dice

½ lb. fresh green beans or
asparagus, trimmed

2 Roma tomatoes, peeled,
deseeded, in small dice

¼ to ½ bunch cilantro, chopped

1 Tbsp. chopped fresh
Italian flat-leaf parsley

5 Tbsp. extra-virgin olive oil

3 cloves garlic, thinly sliced

½ onion, in small dice

1 to 2 Tbsp. fresh lemon juice

1 Tbsp. smoked paprika

2 tsp. unsalted butter

LING COD

1 Tbsp. olive oil

4 pieces ling cod, skin on,
each 5 oz.

1 Tbsp. unsalted butter

LING COD is an underrated West Coast fish whose dense flesh takes well to grilling and, as in this recipe, pan-roasting.
Serves 4

CLAM VINAIGRETTE: Place a saucepan on medium-high heat, then add clams and vermouth. Cover with a lid and steam for 2 to 3 minutes, until clams open.

Drain clams and set aside the cooking liquid in the refrigerator. Discard any clams that do not open. Remove meat from the shells and place in a large stainless steel bowl. Discard shells. Cover and refrigerate clam meat until needed.

Place potato in a saucepan and add enough cold salted water to cover. Cook on medium heat for 4 to 5 minutes, until tender. Use a slotted spoon to transfer potato to paper towels and spread out to cool. In the same cooking water, blanch green beans for 4 minutes, until tender-crisp. Drain and place in a bowl to cool.

To clam meat, add potato, tomatoes, cilantro and parsley.

Heat 3 Tbsp. of the oil in a frying pan on medium heat. Gently sauté garlic for 2 to 3 minutes, until golden. Remove from the heat. Transfer garlic to paper towels and drain. Let oil cool, then add garlic and oil to the clam mixture.

To the same frying pan on medium-high heat, add the remaining oil and heat until it smokes. Sauté onion for 5 to 8 minutes, until translucent and tender. Remove from the heat and let cool.

To the clam mixture, add the reserved cooking liquid, onion, lemon juice and paprika. Season with salt and freshly ground black pepper.

LING COD: Heat oil in a heavy frying pan on medium-high heat. Season fish with salt and pepper, then cook, skin side down, for 6 to 7 minutes, until flesh is just firm. Add butter to the pan, turn fish over and sear briefly for 40 to 45 seconds.

FINISH CLAM VINAIGRETTE: Heat clam vinaigrette in a saucepan on medium heat.

Melt butter in a frying pan on medium heat. Add green beans and cook for 2 minutes, until just tender and hot.

TO SERVE: Divide clam vinaigrette among individual pasta or soup bowls. Arrange green beans over the clam vinaigrette, then top with a piece of fish.

WINE: Serve with a blend of Sauvignon Blanc and Semillon with subtle vanilla oak from Calliope, or try the Bordeaux ringer, classic Sumac Ridge White Meritage.

Italian Tuna-stuffed Eggs

4 large hard-cooked
eggs, peeled

3 1/2-oz. can olive oil-packed
tuna, drained and mashed

1 Tbsp. mayonnaise

4 anchovy fillets,
cut in half lengthwise

16 capers

ARE STUFFED EGGS hokey? You bet! Does Karen care? Nope, not when they're this good! Serve these eggs immediately or refrigerate them for 3 to 4 hours and serve chilled. *Serves 4*

Cut eggs in half lengthwise. Scoop out yolks and press them through a sieve or place in a bowl and mash with a fork. Mix in tuna and mayonnaise, then season with salt and pepper. Stuff the egg halves with the tuna mixture.

TO SERVE: Set egg halves on a chilled plate. Cross 2 anchovy halves on top of each egg half and garnish with capers.

WINE: Gray Monk Siegerrebe has hints of Muscat with full soft fruit texture.

Spicy Spinach Purée

1 lb. spinach, washed
and stemmed

2 Tbsp. unsalted butter

1 cup finely chopped onion

1 tsp. minced garlic

1 Tbsp. minced fresh ginger

2 green chili peppers,
deseeded and finely chopped

1/2 cup diced tomatoes

1/2 tsp. cayenne pepper

1/2 tsp. garam masala

1/2 tsp. turmeric

4 Tbsp. whipping cream

INDIAN FOOD LOVERS will recognize this recipe as one of the classics. It's one of Karen's favourite spinach dishes. *Serves 4*

Place spinach in a large pot on medium-high heat. Steam with just the water that clings to its leaves for 2 to 3 minutes, until tender. Remove from the heat and let cool. Purée in a food processor or blender.

Melt butter in a frying pan on medium heat. Sauté onion, garlic, ginger and chili peppers for 10 minutes, until lightly browned. Add tomatoes and stir briefly. Stir in cayenne, garam masala and turmeric. Add spinach and mix well. Simmer on medium-low heat until spinach becomes very soft and thickens. Season with sea salt and pepper.

TO SERVE: Serve in a bowl as a side dish and drizzle with cream.

Chicken Stew in the Style of Fish Soup

AÏOLI

½ tsp. salt

3 cloves garlic, minced

3 large egg yolks

1 cup extra-virgin olive oil

4 tsp. lemon juice

STEW

4 lbs. chicken thighs,
bone-in and skinless

2 Tbsp. extra-virgin olive oil

1 cup finely diced onion

3 large leeks, white and light
green parts only, thinly sliced

⅔ cup finely diced fennel bulb

4 cloves garlic, minced

3 cups well drained,
finely chopped, canned plum
tomatoes (one 28 oz. can)

3 cups chicken stock or water

2 cups dry white wine

Large pinch of saffron

2 bay leaves

1 tsp. fennel seeds

½ tsp. dried crushed chilies

2 small sprigs fresh thyme

1 strip fresh orange rind

2 Tbsp. finely chopped parsley

THIS RECIPE is based on bouillabaisse, the Provençal fish stew flavoured with tomatoes, saffron and fennel, and enriched with aïoli. These flavours also complement chicken, and this dish is much less intimidating to make than bouillabaisse. This recipe is not only easy to make but also is elegant enough to serve to guests. *Serves 6*

AÏOLI: Place salt and garlic in a small bowl. Use the back of a spoon to mash them together until they form a paste.

Place egg yolks in a food processor or blender, then add the garlic paste. With the motor running, slowly add olive oil until it is completely incorporated and the aïoli is emulsified. If the mixture becomes too thick, add a drop or two of water. Add the lemon juice, then pulse to combine. Cover with plastic wrap and refrigerate; will keep for up to 3 days.

STEW: Season chicken with salt and freshly ground black pepper. Heat 1 Tbsp. of the oil in a frying pan on medium heat. Cook chicken in batches, for 5 minutes per side, until golden brown. Transfer to a plate.

Heat the remaining oil in a heavy saucepan on medium heat. Sauté onion, leeks, fennel and garlic, stirring occasionally, for 4 to 5 minutes, until soft but not brown. Add tomatoes and cook, stirring frequently, for about 15 minutes, until most of the liquid has evaporated. Add stock, wine, saffron, bay leaves, fennel seeds, chilies, thyme and orange peel. Add chicken and any juices that may have flowed out onto the plate. Season lightly with salt and pepper. Cover with a lid and turn down the heat to low, then simmer for 35 to 40 minutes, until chicken is tender and cooked through. Transfer chicken to a clean plate. Skim off and discard fat from the cooking liquid, then turn up the heat to high and boil for 5 minutes. Return chicken to the saucepan and remove from the heat.

TO SERVE: Reheat the stew on medium heat and bring it to a vigorous simmer. Stir in parsley. Ladle into individual serving bowls. Serve with aïoli in a bowl on the side.

WINE: Sip a glass of Jackson-Triggs popular Proprietors' Reserve Merlot.

Marinated Duck Breast with Asian Pear Chutney

FOR A TASTIER CHUTNEY, try to make it a day ahead so the flavours can develop, then reheat it before serving. *Serves 4*

CHUTNEY: Combine sugar and water in a saucepan on medium heat. Cook, shaking the pan gently but not stirring the contents, for about 5 minutes, until sugar has melted. (Stirring may cause sugar to crystallize before it caramelizes.) Add pears, onion and ginger, then cook for 5 minutes, until onion begins to soften. Add chili pepper, vinegar and butter, then cook for 5 minutes, until pears are tender and most of the liquid has evaporated. Remove from the heat.

DUCK: Combine sambal oelek, garlic, ginger, wine, oil and green onions in a nonreactive bowl. Add duck breasts and turn to coat well with the marinade. Cover bowl with plastic wrap and marinate duck in the refrigerator overnight.

Preheat the oven to 350°F. Remove duck from the marinade and pat semi-dry with paper towels. Season with salt. Use a sharp knife to score the skin of duck breasts in a cross-hatch pattern about ⅛-inch deep. Do not pierce the flesh.

Heat oil in an ovenproof pan on medium-high heat. Sear duck breasts, skin side down, for 5 to 8 minutes, until most of the fat is rendered and the skin is crisp. (Turn down the heat, if necessary, to avoid burning the skin.) Pour off and discard any excess fat. Turn over duck, then roast in the oven for 7 to 10 minutes, until cooked medium-rare or medium. Transfer to a cutting board to rest for about 8 minutes.

TO SERVE: Gently reheat the chutney. Cut duck breasts lengthwise into slices ⅓-inch thick and arrange them on a platter or on individual plates. Serve warmed chutney on the side.

WINE: CedarCreek Platinum Reserve Pinot Noir with concentrated cherry and mocha spice is divine with duck.

CHUTNEY

⅓ cup brown sugar

1 tsp. water

2 Asian pears, diced

2 Tbsp. finely diced onion

1 tsp. finely chopped fresh ginger

¼ tsp. finely chopped chili pepper, red or green

¼ cup Japanese rice vinegar

1 Tbsp. unsalted butter

DUCK

½ tsp. sambal oelek

6 cloves garlic, chopped

2 Tbsp. crushed fresh ginger

¼ cup Cabernet Sauvignon or other dry red wine

¼ cup olive oil

2 green onions, thinly sliced

4 duck breast halves, each 8 oz.

2 tsp. vegetable oil

Marinated Duck Breast with Asian Pear Chutney

Grilled Vegetable Terrine
with Oven-roasted Tomato Compote

GRILL THE VEGETABLES under a broiler or on a barbecue at medium-high heat. The eggplant, zucchini and mushrooms can also be cooked on a griddle. Whichever method you choose, the idea is to give the vegetables some colour by grilling or broiling them, which also softens them and brings out their flavour. Baking the terrine in the oven cooks the vegetables.

When you assemble the terrine, you may want to place the green beans lengthwise, end to end, to create attractive green circles among the other vegetables. *Yields 25 slices*

COMPOTE: Preheat the oven to 200°F to 220°F. Place tomato halves on a parchment-lined cookie sheet. Brush with the 1 tsp. of oil and sprinkle with thyme. Bake in the oven for about 2 hours, until partly dried but still soft.

Place tomato halves (you may roughly cut them into large pieces) in a bowl. Add the 4 Tbsp. of oil, lemon juice, salt and pepper, then mix until combined. Refrigerate until needed; will keep for up to 2 days.

VEGETABLES: Preheat the broiler. Brush a little of the oil on red and yellow bell peppers, then place them on a cookie sheet. Broil until the skins blister and begin to char, turning them occasionally to blacken all sides. Transfer to a bowl and cover with a plate. Let cool. Remove skin and seeds, then cut into 3¼-inch strips. Leave the broiler on.

Use a mandoline to slice eggplants and zucchini lengthwise into strips ⅛-inch thick. Brush strips with some of the oil, then place them on a griddle pan on the stove. Cook each side for 1 to 2 minutes, until they take on a little colour. Transfer to a plate.

Brush mushrooms with some of the oil and place them on a cookie sheet. Broil for 2 to 3 minutes, until browned but not yet releasing their liquid. Transfer to a plate. Leave the broiler on.

Brush leeks with the remaining oil and place them on a cookie sheet. Broil for 2 to 3 minutes, until they begin to soften. Transfer to a plate.

Fill a large bowl with ice water. Bring a large pot of salted water to a boil. Plunge green beans into the boiling water and cook for about 4 minutes, until tender. Drop green beans into ice water for 5 minutes, then drain and pat dry. *continued overleaf >*

COMPOTE

2 plum tomatoes, blanched and skinned, cut in half lengthwise

1 tsp. olive oil

2 sprigs fresh thyme, leaves only

4 Tbsp. extra-virgin olive oil

1 Tbsp. fresh lemon juice

VEGETABLES

4 Tbsp. olive oil

4 red bell peppers

4 yellow bell peppers

4 Japanese eggplants

4 zucchini

3 portobello mushrooms, destemmed

2 leeks, split lengthwise and cleaned

4 oz. green beans

TERRINE

3 oz. cream cheese, softened

2 eggs

2¼ tsp. salt

1 tsp. freshly
ground white pepper

1 envelope Knox gelatine

TERRINE: Preheat the oven to 400°F. Line a terrine pan 11½ × 3¼ × 2¾ inches high with plastic wrap, leaving enough hanging over the edges to cover the contents when filled.

Beat cream cheese in an electric mixer with a paddle attachment on medium speed until smooth. Beat in eggs, salt and pepper. Brush the bottom of the terrine pan with a little of the cream cheese mixture.

Layer the grilled vegetables in the terrine pan in the following order: half of the bell peppers, half of the eggplant, half of the green beans, half of the leeks, half of the zucchini, all the mushrooms, the rest of the zucchini, the rest of the leeks, the rest of the green beans and the rest of the eggplant. On top of each layer, brush a little of the cream cheese mixture and sprinkle with the gelatine granules. Finish with a layer of the remaining bell peppers. Fold the plastic wrap over the top of the contents. Cover the terrine pan with a double layer of heavy aluminum foil, making sure that the foil is snugly wrapped around the edges.

Place the terrine pan in a large roasting pan and add enough hot water to reach one third of the way up the sides of the terrine pan. Bake in the oven for about 75 minutes, until the internal temperature reaches at least 180°F. Remove from the oven and take out the terrine pan from the roasting pan.

Place a piece of cardboard underneath the terrine pan and use a pencil to trace around the base. Use scissors to cut out a piece just slightly smaller than the tracing. Cover the cardboard cutout with plastic wrap, then place it on top of the terrine. Place several weights (cans of tomatoes or beans work well) on top of the cardboard. Refrigerate the weighted terrine overnight.

Remove the weights, unwrap the terrine and carefully invert it onto a plate. Cover and refrigerate until needed; will keep for up to 4 days.

TO SERVE: Use a very sharp knife to cut the terrine into slices ½- to ¾-inch thick. Arrange the slices on a serving platter or individual plates. Serve the tomato compote on the side.

WINE: Hillside Estate Pinot Gris Special Reserve Series shows citric apple flavours with appealing intensity.

Leek and Potato Dauphinoise

DAUPHINOISE IS a classic French presentation of the more homey scalloped potatoes. Although there are many variations of this dish, most contain grated cheese. For best results, make this dish a day ahead. Serve with poultry or veal. *Serves 6*

Preheat the oven to 350°F. Line an 8- or 9-inch square ovenproof pan with parchment paper. Cut a square of cardboard to fit inside the pan and wrap it in a piece of aluminum foil.

Place cream in a saucepan on medium-low heat and cook for about 10 minutes, until reduced by one third. Remove from the heat and let cool.

Fill a saucepan with water and bring to a boil on high heat. Add leeks and blanch for 3 minutes. Drain well.

Fill a bowl with water and a dash of salt. Add potatoes and let sit for 5 minutes. Drain potatoes and pat dry. Place potatoes in a bowl and toss gently with melted butter.

To the cream, add leeks, egg yolks, mace and thyme. Stir well to combine.

Cover the bottom of the prepared ovenproof pan with one third of the potatoes. Cover with one third of the cream mixture, then one third of the cheese. Repeat this layering two more times, so that you have 3 layers of each. Bake in the oven for 90 minutes, until potatoes are fork-tender.

Remove from the oven and place the foil-covered square over the contents. Place several weights (cans of tomatoes and beans work well) on top of the cardboard. Let cool to room temperature, then refrigerate the weighted dauphinoise overnight.

Remove the weights and the foil-covered square. Run a knife around the edges of the dauphinoise, then invert the pan onto a cutting board. Unmould the dauphinoise and remove the parchment paper. Cut dauphinoise into squares or triangles.

TO SERVE: Preheat the oven to 325°F. Place the dauphinoise pieces on a baking pan, garnish with grated cheese and gently reheat in the oven for 10 to 15 minutes.

WINE: Serve this creamy side dish with a soft Pinot Gris from Naramata grapes, a Pinot Noir from Similkameen cherries, a herbal Merlot or a cranberry-styled Cabernet Sauvignon from Morning Bay, the new Pender Island producer.

2 cups whipping cream

1 large leek, white and light green part only, in 1-inch dice

2¼ lbs. Yukon Gold potatoes, thinly sliced

¼ cup clarified butter, melted

2 egg yolks

¼ tsp. mace

½ tsp. fresh thyme leaves

2 cups grated Grana Padano or Parmesan cheese, plus additional for garnish

Tangerine Glaze and Peppered Fig Sauce

GLAZE

2 tangerines,
zest of, julienned

2 Tbsp. sugar

1 cinnamon stick, 1-inch long

½ star anise

1 berry allspice

Pinch of mace

2 Tbsp. honey

1 cup fresh tangerine juice

SAUCE

3 oz. dried figs

¼ cup Madeira

2 Tbsp. sugar

½ tsp. crushed black pepper

1 clove

2 Tbsp. honey

2 Tbsp. sherry vinegar

3 cups chicken stock

1 Tbsp. butter (optional)

THIS GLAZE and sauce are perfect accompaniments to duck, Cornish game hens or pork. Serve the glazed dish with the peppered fig sauce.

Use fresh figs when they are in season, instead of dried. Cook the sauce without the figs, then add ½ cup of fresh figs, diced or quartered, just before serving. If you make your own chicken stock for this recipe, brown the bones first to give the stock more colour. *Serves 6*

GLAZE: Bring a small saucepan of water to a boil on high heat. Add tangerine zest, blanch for 1 minute, then drain. Blanch zest 2 more times, using a fresh pot of water each time. Drain.

Place sugar in a small saucepan on medium heat and cook until it melts and just begins to turn golden. Gently stir in cinnamon, star anise, allspice, mace and honey. Cook for 5 minutes, until colour deepens a bit to amber. Slowly and carefully stir in tangerine juice, then cook for about 12 minutes, until reduced to half or to a glazing thickness. Strain through a fine-mesh sieve into a clean bowl and discard the solids.

SAUCE: Place figs and Madeira in a small bowl and let soak for 24 hours.

Place sugar in a small saucepan on medium heat, then cook until it melts and just begins to turn golden. Add figs, Madeira, pepper, clove and honey, then toss gently and cook until sugar melts again. Add vinegar and deglaze the saucepan. Stir in stock and bring to a boil, then turn down the heat to low and simmer for 1 hour, until the sauce is the consistency of jam. Strain sauce through a fine-mesh sieve into a clean bowl and discard the solids.

TO SERVE: Brush the glaze over meat just before you finish cooking it. Return to the oven to cook for 5 minutes.

Reheat the sauce gently. To make it shiny and more luxurious, whisk in butter (optional) while reheating. Serve sauce on the side.

WINE: Nichol Vineyard Syrah from the Naramata Bench with its brandied cherries character suits the cinnamon, allspice and honey of these side dishes.

Tangerine-glazed Duck with Peppered Fig Sauce

Temari Zushi

Temari Zushi

"TEMARI" are children's rubber bouncing balls, and temari zushi are an easy-to-make sushi that looks like them. The arrangement of the three types of temari zushi is very pretty. The temari can be made up to 3 hours ahead and kept wrapped in plastic. Do not refrigerate them, or the rice will harden and become waxy. The Japanese Kewpie mayonnaise for the crabmeat and avocado temari is sold in Asian specialty stores. *Serves 4*

RICE: Wash rice and discard any chaff or stones, then drain. Place rice and water in a heavy saucepan on high heat, and cover with a lid, then bring to a boil. This should take about 5 minutes. Turn down the heat to low, then simmer for 10 minutes. Turn off the heat and allow rice to sit on the element for another 10 minutes.

While the rice is cooking, combine sugar, salt and vinegar in a bowl. Stir to dissolve sugar and salt.

Transfer cooked rice to a wide shallow bowl and use a wooden spoon to gently fluff it. Drizzle the vinegar mixture over the rice. Continue gently stirring the rice with one hand and fanning it with the other for 5 to 6 minutes, until slightly cooled.

TERIYAKI SAUCE: Mix together water, soy sauce, sugar and sake in a saucepan on medium-low heat. Boil mixture for 5 minutes, until well combined. Be careful not to let it burn. Remove from the heat and let cool. Stir in vinegar, then transfer to a drizzle bottle.

TEMARI 1: Cut a piece of plastic wrap about 10 × 10 inches and place it on a cutting board. Place a strip of smoked salmon in the middle of the plastic wrap. Use your hands to form a small ball of rice about 1½ inches in diameter. Do not pack the rice too firmly. Place the ball of rice on the salmon. Gather up the edges of the plastic wrap around the rice ball, then twist them tightly together to form a compact ball. Unwrap the rice ball and place it on a plate. Repeat the process to make 3 more balls. Top each with a triangle of lemon. *continued overleaf >*

RICE

1 cup short-grain rice

1 cup water

1 tsp. sugar

⅛ tsp. salt

1 Tbsp. balsamic vinegar

TERIYAKI SAUCE

¼ cup water

2 Tbsp. light soy sauce

2 Tbsp. sugar

1 Tbsp. + 1 tsp. sake

1 tsp. balsamic vinegar

TEMARI 1

3 oz. smoked salmon, in 4 strips, 1 × 2 inches

1 slice lemon, in 4 tiny triangles about ⅓ inch at widest part

TEMARI 2

1 egg

1 tsp. vegetable oil

4 nori strips, each about ½ × 4 inches

TEMARI 3

4 tsp. cooked shredded crabmeat

1 tsp. Kewpie or regular mayonnaise

¼ avocado, in 4 thin slices

1 tsp. tobiko (flying fish roe, optional)

TEMARI 2: Place the egg in a bowl and beat lightly. Heat a 10-inch frying pan on medium-high heat. When a drop of water sizzles as it hits the pan, add oil and swirl it around the pan. Add the beaten egg, tilting the pan so the egg forms a thin crepe. Cook for 1 minute, until set. Transfer to a cutting board and cut the crepe into quarters, to make 4 triangles.

Cut a piece of plastic wrap about 10 × 10 inches and place it on a cutting board. Place a strip of nori in the middle of the plastic wrap. Top the nori with a triangle of egg. Use your hands to form a small ball of rice about 1½ inches in diameter and make 4 temari according to the instructions for temari 1.

TEMARI 3: Lightly combine crabmeat and mayonnaise in a bowl.

Cut a piece of plastic wrap about 10 × 10 inches and place it on a cutting board. Set a strip of avocado in the middle of the plastic wrap. Use your hands to form a small ball of rice about 1½ inches in diameter and make 4 temari according to the instructions for temari 1. Top each with some crabmeat and a sprinkle of tobiko (optional).

TO SERVE: Arrange one of each temari on each individual plate. Drizzle the plates with teriyaki sauce.

WINE: Pair with Hawthorne Mountain See Ya Later Pinot Gris.

Ebi Yuba Shinjyo

(Shrimp and Asparagus Rolls)

BEAN CURD SHEETS are about 20 inches in diameter and are sold in Asian grocery stores. You can steam these rolls ahead of time, then refrigerate them in a resealable plastic bag (they will keep for up to 1 day). Heat them in a microwave oven on medium-high heat for 90 seconds before slicing and serving. *Serves 6*

Squeeze out excess moisture from shredded potato, then fluff with your fingers. Heat vegetable oil in a frying on medium-high heat and fry shredded potato in batches for 5 to 8 minutes, until golden and crisp. Use a slotted spoon to remove potato and drain on paper towels.

Place shrimp, green onions, salt, pepper and sesame oil in a blender or food processor. Pulse until finely chopped but not puréed.

Use scissors to cut bean curd sheet into six equal pie-shaped wedges. Spread one sixth of the shrimp mixture along the wide end of a bean curd wedge. Lay a piece of asparagus on top of the shrimp. Brush the point of the bean curd wedge with some beaten egg yolk. Starting at the wide end, roll up the bean curd, making sure that the shrimp filling encases the asparagus. Fill and roll up the remaining bean curd wedges.

Place the rolls in a bamboo or metal steamer. Bring a large pot of water to a boil on high heat. Turn down the heat to a simmer, then place the steamer over the pot. Steam the rolls for 15 minutes, until fairly firm when pressed lightly with a fingertip.

Transfer the rolls to a cutting board. Use a sharp knife to cut off the ragged ends on each roll, then slice each roll into 4 equal pieces.

TO SERVE: Arrange a cluster of 4 pieces of roll on each plate. Garnish with a small haystack of fried potatoes.

WINE: Celebrate with Summerhill Pyramid Winery Cipes Brut, made from Riesling grapes.

1 Yukon Gold potato, finely shredded or julienned

2 Tbsp. vegetable oil

10 to 12 oz. (about 30) fresh raw shrimp, shelled

2 green onions, white part only, trimmed and chopped

½ tsp. salt

¼ tsp. black pepper

1 tsp. sesame oil

1 bean curd sheet

6 stalks asparagus, trimmed and stems peeled if very thick

1 egg yolk, lightly beaten

Small wedge of lemon

Marinated Sablefish

with Garlic-fried Pepper Leaves and Maple-Ginger Drizzle

SABLEFISH

2 Tbsp. citrus soy sauce

1 Tbsp. maple syrup

¼ tsp. sambal oelek

4 pieces sablefish, skinned, each 6 oz.

½ tsp. vegetable oil

PEPPER LEAVES

2 Tbsp. vegetable oil

2 cloves garlic, crushed

8 oz. pepper leaves

DRIZZLE

¼ cup maple syrup

2 Tbsp. butter

1 tsp. grated fresh ginger

CITRUS SOY SAUCE (often labelled "ponzu") is sold in Asian food stores, and it gives the sablefish a real lift. Pepper leaves also are available in Asian markets. If you can't find them, use spinach leaves, Swiss chard leaves or fresh pea greens. *Serves 4*

SABLEFISH: Combine citrus soy sauce, maple syrup and sambal oelek in a nonreactive bowl. Season with salt and freshly ground white pepper. Add fish, cover bowl and marinate in the refrigerator for 1 hour.

PEPPER LEAVES: Heat oil in a wok or large frying pan on medium-high heat. Sauté garlic for 1 minute, until aromatic. Add pepper leaves and cook for about 5 minutes, until wilted but still a bit crunchy. Season with salt and freshly ground white pepper.

DRIZZLE: Combine maple syrup, butter and ginger in a saucepan on medium heat. Bring to a boil, then remove from heat.

FINISH SABLEFISH: Place oil in a nonstick frying pan on medium-high heat. Remove fish from the marinade and pat dry. Discard the marinade. Sear fish for about 2 minutes, until golden. Turn over and cook for 5 to 7 minutes, until just opaque.

TO SERVE: Mound pepper leaves in the middle of each plate. Top with a piece of fish, then drizzle with the sauce.

WINE: Mission Hill Reserve Sauvignon Blanc combines herbs and gooseberry with fresh citrus acidity.

Marinated Sablefish with Garlic-fried Pepper Leaves and Maple-Ginger Drizzle

Prawn and Shiitake Mushroom Gyoza
with Kaffir Lime Butter Sauce

GYOZA

6 oz. prawn meat,
coarsely chopped

2 green onions, sliced

6 shiitake mushrooms,
destemmed and sliced

4 fresh water chestnuts,
peeled, blanched and diced

1 rib celery, minced

1 Tbsp. grated fresh ginger

1 Tbsp. toasted sesame seeds

1 Tbsp. sesame oil

2 Tbsp. soy sauce

1 Tbsp. chopped fresh cilantro

1 tsp. all-purpose flour

24 frozen gyoza or won ton
wrappers, thawed

1 egg, beaten

1 Tbsp. salt

4 sprigs fresh cilantro for garnish

Toasted sesame seeds
for garnish

SAUCE

½ cup Noilly Prat or other
dry white vermouth

1 shallot, thinly sliced

4 kaffir lime leaves, julienned

½ cup unsalted butter, in cubes

1 lime, juice of

Drop of liquid honey

THESE GYOZA can be made ahead of time and frozen. Lay filled gyoza on a parchment-lined cookie sheet and freeze until hard. Transfer the frozen gyoza to an airtight container and store in the freezer for up to 5 days. Thaw frozen gyoza in the refrigerator before cooking them.

If fresh water chestnuts are not available, use canned ones and drain them before dicing. *Serves 4*

GYOZA: Combine prawn meat, green onions, mushrooms, water chestnuts, celery, ginger, sesame seeds, oil, soy sauce and cilantro in a bowl. Mix well, then season with salt and freshly ground white pepper.

Dust a large cookie sheet with flour.

Arrange gyoza wrappers on a cool dry surface in 2 rows of 12. Lightly brush the edges of each wrapper with beaten egg. Place a twelfth of the filling in the middle of 12 wrappers. Cover each one with the remaining wrappers, egg side down. Use your fingers to press around the edges of each gyoza, one side at a time, to get rid of any trapped air and to seal in the filling. Be sure to seal the gyoza well. Place them on the prepared cookie sheet, then refrigerate for up to 1 hour.

SAUCE: Combine vermouth, shallot and kaffir lime leaves in a saucepan on high heat. Bring to a boil, then turn down the heat to medium-low. Carefully whisk in butter, then remove the saucepan from the heat. (Be careful not to let this butter sauce boil, or it will split.) Stir in lime juice and honey. Season with salt and freshly ground white pepper. Keep warm.

FINISH GYOZA: Place 16 cups of water in a stockpot on high heat and bring to a rapid boil, then add salt. Drop gyoza into the water and cook for about 2 minutes, until they float to the top. Cook them for another 30 seconds.

TO SERVE: Use a slotted spoon to transfer 3 gyoza to each bowl or plate, then spoon warm butter sauce over them. Garnish with a sprig of cilantro and toasted sesame seeds.

WINE: Try CedarCreek Estate Select Pinot Blanc (Greata Ranch), or the fresh Pinot Blanc from Blue Mountain.

Smoked Clam Salad

Smoked Clam Salad

CLAMS

2 lbs. clams

1 tsp. sugar

1 tsp. chili powder

2 Tbsp. olive oil

Hickory chips (enough to cover bottom of wok or barbecue)

MARINADE

1 shallot, finely chopped

1 tsp. minced capers

1 tsp. minced sweet dill pickle

2 Tbsp. finely chopped fresh parsley

2 Tbsp. olive oil

1 Tbsp. Dijon mustard

SALAD

1 cup small broccoli florets

1 zucchini, in ¼-inch slices

1 cup small cauliflower florets

2 carrots, in 2 × ¼-inch sticks

6 stalks asparagus, trimmed, stems cut in 1-inch lengths but tips left whole

12 snow peas, strings removed

18 green beans, cut in thirds

¼ cup French dressing or light vinaigrette

IF YOU DO NOT HAVE a wok, you can smoke clams on the barbecue. Cover the bottom of the barbecue with hickory chips. Place the clams in their half shells on a perforated pizza pan, or on aluminum foil with holes poked in it. When the hickory chips start to smoke, place the clams on the barbecue for a few minutes.

For a more formal presentation, save half of the clam shells, place them in a bowl, cover and refrigerate until serving. Arrange the clam meat in the half shells. *Serves 4 to 6*

CLAMS: Scrub clams well, then place in a large bowl of cold water and soak overnight in the refrigerator. Tap clams lightly with a knife and discard any clams that stay open.

Fill a large saucepan with 1 cup water and bring to a boil on high heat. Add clams, cover with a lid and steam for 6 minutes, until shells open. Remove from heat. Discard any clams that have not opened. Use a knife to remove half of the shell from each clam. Discard the half shells without the meat. Combine sugar, chili powder and oil in a bowl and drizzle over each clam.

Cover the bottom of a wok with hickory chips, then set the clams in their half shells on top. Cover with a lid and place the wok on medium heat. When the chips start to smoke (make sure the exhaust fan is on), cook clams for 2 minutes. Remove clams from heat, then detach meat from the half shells.

MARINADE: Combine all of the ingredients in a nonreactive bowl. Add clam meat, cover the bowl and marinate overnight in the refrigerator.

SALAD: Bring a large pot of water to a boil on high heat. Blanch broccoli, zucchini, cauliflower, carrots, asparagus, snow peas and green beans until they are just tender. Drain, place in a bowl and toss with dressing.

TO SERVE: Arrange vegetables in the middle of a serving platter. Arrange clam meat around the vegetables, then drizzle with some of the marinade.

WINE: Sip La Frenz Winery's Alexandria of late-picked Muscat first as an aperitif, then to accompany the sugar and chili powder in this dish.

Tarte à l'Oignon à l'Alsacienne
(Alsatian Onion Tart)

A TRUE CLASSIC, this tart makes a savoury starter for a meal or an excellent lunch with a green salad. If you are in a hurry, heat the milk before adding it to the flour, as when the milk is hot, you can add it all in one go. *Serves 6 to 8*

Lightly flour a work surface. Roll out pastry to a thickness of ⅛ inch, in a round big enough to line a 10-inch tart pan or pie plate. Pat pastry into place in the pan and chill in the refrigerator while you make the filling.

Heat oil in a frying pan on medium heat and cook onions, stirring occasionally, for 30 to 40 minutes, until tender but not browned. Drain in a fine-mesh sieve and discard pan juices. Place onions in a bowl.

Preheat the oven to 375°F.

Melt butter in a saucepan on medium heat. Whisk in flour and cook, stirring, for 2 to 3 minutes. Slowly whisk in milk. Remove from the heat and pour over the onions. Whisk in eggs, cream, nutmeg and bacon. Season with salt and pepper.

Pour the onion mixture into the chilled pastry. Bake in the oven for 30 to 35 minutes, until golden on top and pastry is cooked. Remove from the oven and let cool for 5 minutes before serving.

TO SERVE: Cut into wedges and serve a warm wedge on each plate.

WINE: Serve Blue Mountain Pinot Gris (or the Reserve "Stripe Label"), or the complex true varietal Pinot Reach Old Vines Riesling.

12 oz. short-crust pastry

1 Tbsp. vegetable oil

3 large onions, thinly sliced

6 Tbsp. butter

6 Tbsp. all-purpose flour

1 cup milk

4 eggs, lightly beaten

1 cup whipping cream

Dash of nutmeg

3 to 4 slices bacon, blanched, in 1-inch strips

{ LE CROCODILE: *michel jacob* }

Tarte à l'Oignon à l'Alsacienne

Crispy Cheese Wafers

YOU CAN VARY this basic recipe by topping the cooled wafers with a piece of Stilton cheese and half a walnut (omit sprinkling with almond powder), then placing them in the oven to melt the cheese. Serve the wafers with a glass of Champagne before dinner, or use them to garnish a salad. *Yields 18 wafers*

⅓ cup skinless toasted almonds

¾ cup all-purpose flour

6 Tbsp. + 2 tsp. unsalted butter, cold, in cubes

1 egg yolk

4 oz. Gruyère, grated

Pinch of cayenne pepper

Pinch of salt and freshly ground black pepper

1 egg beaten with 1 Tbsp. cold water

In a food processor fitted with a steel blade, grind almonds to a fine powder, but be careful not to let it turn into butter. Transfer to a small bowl.

Place flour, butter, egg yolk, cheese, cayenne, salt and black pepper in the food processor. Mix until the dough forms a ball.

Preheat the oven to 350°F. Line a cookie sheet with parchment paper.

Roll out the dough on a lightly floured surface to a thickness of ⅛ inch, in a rectangle about 7 × 12 inches. Cut it into strips 1 × 4 inches. Place wafers on the prepared cookie sheet, leaving a little space between them, and refrigerate for 20 minutes.

Brush wafers with the beaten egg mixture, then sprinkle with almond powder. Bake in the oven for about 15 minutes, until golden. Remove from the oven and cool on a wire rack.

TO SERVE: Serve these delicate wafers warm from the oven or at room temperature.

WINE: Blue Mountain Gold Label Sparkling Brut makes a great celebratory start.

Herb-crusted Lamb Chops with Herb Jus

SERVE THESE lamb chops with a fresh vegetable ratatouille.
Serves 4

HERB CRUST

2 cups fresh bread crumbs

1 large handful of fresh
Italian flat-leaf parsley

2 Tbsp. fresh thyme leaves

2 Tbsp. chopped fresh rosemary

1 clove garlic, finely chopped

6 Tbsp. olive oil

LAMB

4 thick loin lamb chops,
frenched, each 6 to 8 oz.

1 Tbsp. olive oil

2 Tbsp. Dijon mustard

JUS

1 cup Cabernet Sauvignon
or other dry red wine

1 sprig thyme

1 sprig rosemary

1 tsp. finely chopped garlic

¼ cup chilled butter, in cubes

HERB CRUST: Place bread crumbs, parsley, thyme, rosemary, garlic and oil in a food processor. Mix for 60 seconds, until the mixture sticks together when pressed between finger and thumb.

LAMB: Preheat the oven to 375°F. Season lamb with salt and pepper.

Heat oil in a heavy ovenproof frying pan on medium-high heat until nearly smoking. Sear lamb on all sides for 3 to 4 minutes, until well browned. Brush with mustard, then coat with the herb crust. Roast in the oven for 5 minutes. For medium or well-done, cook the lamb longer. Remove from the oven and transfer to a warmed serving platter. Let lamb rest for 10 minutes. Save the frying pan.

JUS: Place the reserved frying pan on medium-high heat. Add wine and deglaze the pan, scraping up all of the brown bits from the bottom. Add thyme, rosemary and garlic, then cook for about 10 minutes, until the jus is reduced to one third. Strain through a fine-mesh sieve into a saucepan. Just before serving, slowly whisk butter, one piece at a time, into the warm jus.

TO SERVE: Place a chop on each plate and drizzle with warm jus.

WINE: Relish the complex intensity of the Meritage blend from Osoyoos Larose, or the minty Cabernet Sauvignon or dark plum Merlot from La Frenz Winery.

Herb-crusted Lamb Chops with Herb Jus

Shortbread Cookies

with Macerated Berries and Warm Sabayon

FRUIT

2 cups wild berries

2 Tbsp. Grand Marnier

½ orange, zest of

COOKIES

1 lb. butter, softened

1 cup sugar

3½ cups all-purpose flour

SABAYON

5 egg yolks

½ lemon, zest of, finely grated

½ cup sugar

1 cup icewine

THESE SHORTBREAD COOKIES are also delicious on their own. If you do not have wild berries, use fresh fruit such as peaches, apricots or cherries. Blanch the peaches and apricots first, then remove and discard the skins and the pits; pit the cherries. Cut the fruit into ½-inch slices or 1-inch cubes.

If icewine is unavailable, use a dessert wine such as Madeira, Marsala, Beaume de Venise or sweet sherry. *Serves 4*

FRUIT: Gently combine wild berries, Grand Marnier and orange zest in a stainless steel bowl. Let sit at room temperature for 2 hours.

COOKIES: Preheat the oven to 400°F. Line a cookie sheet with parchment paper.

Cream butter in an electric mixer until smooth and light. Slowly add sugar, beating until very well combined. Add flour, a bit at a time, then mix with your hands until the dough forms a ball. (Add more flour if the dough is too soft.)

Place the dough on a lightly floured surface, flatten it, then roll it out to a thickness of ½ inch. Cut into desired shapes and place on the prepared cookie sheet. Bake in the oven for 8 to 10 minutes, until bottoms are light golden brown. Remove from the oven and place on a wire rack to cool.

SABAYON: Place egg yolks, lemon zest and sugar in a stainless steel bowl. Whisk until the mixture is thick and pale. Place the bowl over a saucepan of simmering but not boiling water on lowest heat. Slowly add icewine, whisking constantly, for about 10 minutes, until the mixture is thick and frothy.

TO SERVE: Divide fruit among individual bowls and top with warm sabayon. Serve with a shortbread cookie on the side. Arrange the remaining cookies on a plate to pass around.

WINE: Honeyed Mt. Boucherie Estate Winery Ehrenfelser Late Harvest (with a touch of botrytised Optima) has tropical fruit and figs.

Almond and Garlic-crusted Lamb Loin
with Spring Vegetables and Thyme Jus

THE ALMOND CRUST adds not only texture and flavour to the lamb, it helps to keep the meat juicy. *Serves 4*

CRUST: Place garlic and milk in a saucepan on medium heat. Add a pinch of sea salt, then simmer until garlic is tender. Pour off and discard milk. Place garlic and ground almonds in a food processor and process until they form a fairly smooth paste.

YOGURT SAUCE: Combine yogurt, almond extract and a pinch of sea salt in a bowl.

VEGETABLES: Fill a bowl with ice water. Bring a saucepan of salted water to a boil, then briefly blanch, in separate batches, carrots, snow peas, fava beans, green onions and asparagus, until al dente. Immediately plunge the vegetables into the bowl of ice water, then drain well. Place on paper towels.

POTATOES: Line a cookie sheet with parchment paper. Divide potatoes into 4 equal stacks, then use the palm of your hand to flatten and fan out each stack into a circular pattern of overlapping slices.

Heat oil in a frying pan on medium heat, then cook each potato cake for about 5 minutes per side, until golden and crisp. Season with sea salt and black pepper. Transfer to the prepared cookie sheet.

LAMB: Preheat the oven to 400°F. Line a roasting pan with parchment paper. Season lamb with sea salt and black pepper.

Place oil in a nonstick frying pan on medium-high heat. When hot, sear lamb on all sides for about 5 minutes, until evenly browned. Remove from the heat and let rest for 1 minute. Spread almond-garlic paste over lamb and sprinkle lightly with ground almonds.

Transfer lamb to the roasting pan, then roast in the oven, turning occasionally, for 10 to 15 minutes, until a meat thermometer reads 130°F. Remove from the oven and place on a cutting board to rest for 5 minutes. Leave the oven on.

Place the roasting pan on medium-high heat. Add stock and deglaze the pan. Cook for 3 to 4 minutes, until the jus thickens just a little. Stir in thyme. *continued overleaf >*

CRUST
2 bulbs garlic, separated into cloves, peeled

2 cups milk

1 cup ground almonds

YOGURT SAUCE
2 Tbsp. plain yogurt

4 drops bitter almond extract

VEGETABLES
4 baby carrots, peeled

1 cup snow peas, trimmed

⅓ cup shelled and peeled fava beans,

8 green onions, white part only, trimmed

8 stalks asparagus, trimmed

1 Tbsp. butter

1 tsp. minced fresh thyme leaves

2 Roma tomatoes, peeled, deseeded, cut lengthwise into 4 slices

POTATOES
2 russet potatoes, peeled and cut in ⅛-inch slices

1 Tbsp. extra-virgin olive oil

LAMB
2 lamb loins, each 8 oz.

2 tsp. vegetable oil

2 tsp. ground almonds

¾ cup concentrated lamb or chicken stock

2 tsp. minced fresh thyme leaves

FINISH VEGETABLES: Melt butter in a frying pan on medium heat. Lightly sauté carrots, snow peas, fava beans, green onions and asparagus for 5 minutes, until heated through. Sprinkle with thyme.

FINISH POTATOES: Place potatoes in the oven for about 5 minutes, until warmed through.

TO SERVE: Cut each loin into 4 slices, then place 2 slices on each plate. Set a potato cake beside the lamb and arrange vegetables on top. Drizzle with thyme jus. Garnish each plate a with a slice of tomato and a few drops of yogurt sauce.

WINE: Inniskillin Dark Horse Estate Vineyard Meritage contains mostly Merlot, aged in American and French oak barrels.

Squash and Mascarpone Ravioli
with Truffle Butter

FOR QUICKER and easier preparation, use store-bought fresh pasta sheets or won ton wrappers. If you do not own a ravioli mould, make larger ravioli and cut them by hand, then serve just 1 or 2 pieces per person. *Serves 4*

FILLING: Preheat the oven to 325°F. Line a cookie sheet with parchment paper. Coat the cut sides of squash with a little oil, then season with salt and freshly ground white pepper. Place cut side down on the prepared cookie sheet and bake in the oven for 20 to 30 minutes, until cooked through and soft. Remove from the oven and let cool. Scoop out the flesh and measure out 2 cups. (Freeze the remainder for use in another recipe; will keep for up to 6 months.)

Purée squash, mascarpone and nutmeg in a blender or food processor until very smooth. Press through a fine-mesh sieve, using the back of a wooden spoon or a spatula to remove any lumps. Add Parmesan. Season to taste with salt and freshly ground white pepper. Cover and refrigerate until ready to make ravioli.

RAVIOLI: Divide pasta dough into 8 portions and roll each one through a pasta machine to form a sheet ⅟₁₆-inch thick and large enough to fit a ravioli mould. Sprinkle the inside of the ravioli mould with a little flour to prevent sticking, then line with a sheet of pasta, pressing gently into the spaces. Place the filling in a pastry bag with a round flat tip and pipe about 1 Tbsp. into each square.

Make an egg wash by whisking together egg and water in a bowl. Place another sheet of pasta on a clean surface and use a pastry brush to paint one side of it with egg wash. Carefully place the pastry sheet, egg wash side down, over the filled ravioli. Gently press along the seams to seal the pasta sheets together and to get rid of any air bubbles. Use a floured rolling pin to gently roll over the top sheet to help mould the individual ravioli. Trim off and discard the outside edges. Turn the mould over onto a parchment-lined baking sheet, remove all the ravioli in one piece, then place in the freezer. Repeat process until all the sheets of pasta are used up. *continued overleaf >*

FILLING
2 butternut squash, each 1½ lbs., halved and deseeded

2 tsp. olive oil

4 Tbsp. mascarpone cheese

½ tsp. ground nutmeg

2 Tbsp. freshly grated Parmesan cheese

RAVIOLI
1¼ lbs. pasta dough (page 151), omit the saffron

1 egg

½ tsp. water

⅓ cup rice vinegar

2 Tbsp. dry white wine

1 tsp. whipping cream (optional)

⅓ cup chilled
unsalted butter, cubed

1 Tbsp. fresh lemon juice

¼ tsp. white truffle oil

1 Tbsp. finely chopped
black truffle or
¼ tsp. white truffle oil

After being frozen, the ravioli in each mould will be easy to break apart (each mould makes 10 ravioli). No cutting is necessary if done properly. (The ravioli can be made ahead up to this point. Place in an airtight container; will keep in the freezer for up to 2½ weeks.) Do not thaw before cooking.

SAUCE: Combine vinegar and wine in a saucepan on medium heat, then cook for 2 to 3 minutes, until they form a light syrup. (If you are not experienced at making butter sauces, you can prevent the sauce from splitting by adding the optional cream.) Turn down the heat to low, then whisk in butter, a piece at a time, until well incorporated. Do not boil. Stir in lemon juice, truffle oil and chopped truffle. Season to taste with salt. Keep warm by placing the saucepan in a larger pan of hot water. When reheating, be careful not to boil the sauce, as it may split.

TO SERVE: Bring a stockpot with 24 cups of salted water to a boil, add frozen ravioli and cook for 3 to 4½ minutes, until al dente. Place 4 to 10 ravioli on each plate. Spoon warm truffle sauce over the ravioli.

WINE: Serve with buttery Quails' Gate Family Reserve Chardonnay aged in French oak with extended lees contact, or with another treasured white.

Pork in Brine

SERVE THIS DISH with puréed potatoes and caramelized apple rings. *Serves 6*

PORK: Make the brine by combining water, sugar and salt in a stockpot on high heat. Bring to a boil, then remove from the heat and immediately add celery, carrots, onion, bay leaves and peppercorns. Let cool.

Place pork chops in a bowl and add brine. Cover and refrigerate for 48 hours. Remove from the refrigerator 30 minutes before cooking.

Preheat the oven to 450°F. Remove pork chops from brine and pat dry with paper towels. Discard the brine.

Heat oil in a frying pan on high heat. Sear pork chops, one at a time, for 3 to 4 minutes per side, until a dark caramel colour. Place on a baking sheet and roast in the oven for about 10 minutes for medium-rare (150°F on a meat thermometer). Let rest for 5 minutes before serving.

SAUCE: Heat oil in a frying pan on medium heat and sauté bacon for about 3 minutes. Turn up the heat to high, add 2 Tbsp. of the butter, then sauté mushrooms for about 10 minutes, until dark golden brown. Add pearl onions and cook for 5 minutes, until they can be pierced with a sharp knife. Add stock and cook until reduced to half. Taste and adjust seasoning. Remove from the heat, then whisk in the remaining butter and herbs.

TO SERVE: Place a pork chop on each plate and spoon some sauce over it.

WINE: Inniskillin Merlot Reserve from the Okanagan Valley with its long, round and toasty finish is a nice match.

PORK

16 cups water

2/3 cup sugar

2/3 cup salt

3 ribs celery, roughly chopped

2 carrots, roughly chopped

1 onion, roughly chopped

2 bay leaves

2 Tbsp. black peppercorns

6 pork chops, each 8 oz.

1 Tbsp. vegetable oil

SAUCE

2 Tbsp. vegetable oil

¼ cup chopped bacon

¼ cup unsalted butter

2 lbs. button mushrooms, halved

12 pearl onions, blanched and peeled

3 cups chicken stock

¼ cup chopped mixed fresh herbs (thyme, parsley, chives)

{ LUMIÈRE: *rob feenie* }

Lemon Coeur à la Crème with Lemon Sauce

Lemon Coeur à la Crème with Lemon Sauce

TURBINADO SUGAR has a coarse texture and is light brown in colour because it contains a small amount of molasses. It is available in most specialty food stores and health food stores.

This recipe calls for vanilla seeds only. Save the husk, tightly wrapped in plastic and stored in the refrigerator, for another use. *Serves 8*

FROMAGE BLANC: Purée yogurt and cottage cheese in a blender until very smooth. Stir in lemon juice. Transfer to an airtight container and refrigerate for at least 24 hours before using. Makes about 2 cups. (You will be using 1 cup; the rest will keep in the refrigerator for up to 1 week.)

COEUR À LA CRÈME: Chill a bowl in the freezer. Cut eight pieces of cheesecloth 6 inches square, large enough to line the insides of eight ½-cup ramekins with an extra inch to cover the filling. Soak the cheesecloth in ice water for at least 25 minutes.

Combine turbinado sugar and lemon juice in a saucepan on medium heat and cook until it reaches 220°F on a candy thermometer. Remove lemon syrup from the heat and let cool.

In the chilled bowl, whip cream and vanilla seeds until soft peaks form.

In another bowl, gently stir mascarpone to soften it. Pass 1 cup of the fromage blanc through a sieve (this makes it fluffy and easier to incorporate into the mascarpone). Slowly add fromage blanc to mascarpone, stirring gently to ensure there are no lumps. Drizzle in the lemon syrup and mix well. Fold in whipped cream.

Squeeze excess water from the cheesecloth squares and fit them tightly into the ramekins, ensuring all of the inside surfaces are covered, with an inch excess over the sides. Spoon coeur à la crème into ramekins until full. Fold the excess cheesecloth over the contents of the filled ramekins and gently push down on the top to ensure the coeur à la crème takes the shape of the ramekins. Refrigerate for at least 6 hours. *continued overleaf >*

FROMAGE BLANC
1 cup yogurt
1 cup cottage cheese
1½ tsp. fresh lemon juice

COEUR À LA CRÈME
½ cup turbinado sugar
¼ cup fresh lemon juice
½ cup whipping cream
½ vanilla bean, seeds only
2 cups mascarpone cheese
1 cup fromage blanc

SAUCE

6 egg yolks

1¼ cups sugar

½ cup + 1 Tbsp. fresh lemon juice

⅓ cup unsalted butter,
softened

SAUCE: Fill a bowl with ice. Whisk together egg yolks, sugar, lemon juice and butter in a stainless steel bowl. Mix well. Place the bowl over a saucepan of simmering but not boiling water on medium heat. Cook for about 20 minutes, stirring occasionally, until the sauce is thick enough to coat the back of a spoon. Place over the bowl of ice to stop the cooking. Let cool, stirring from time to time. Strain through a fine-mesh sieve, then place in a covered container and refrigerate until needed.

TO SERVE: Undo the cheesecloth at the top of each ramekin. Invert each ramekin onto an individual plate, gently lifting up the ramekin and pulling down on the cheesecloth to free the coeur à la crème. Pour 1 or 2 Tbsp. of the lemon sauce over each one.

WINE: Domaine Combret has a special Seville orange and lemon character in icewines of either Chardonnay or Gamay grapes.

Murch Hyderabadi

(Chicken from Hyderabad)

THIS IS a mild chicken curry. We use ghee, or clarified butter, in this recipe. It is available from Indian markets. Although ¾ cup ghee is traditional in this recipe, you can use as little as ⅓ cup. Garnish this curry with tamarind chutney and serve it with rice or *naan* (Indian bread). *Serves 6*

Place ¼ cup of the stock, ginger, garlic paste, chili flakes and turmeric in a bowl. Stir well to combine.

Heat ghee in a frying pan on medium heat. Cook onions, stirring occasionally, for 15 to 20 minutes, until golden brown. Stir in the seasoned stock and cook for 1 minute. Add chicken and the remaining chicken stock. Bring to a boil, then turn down the heat to low and simmer for about 20 minutes, until chicken is tender. Season with salt. Sprinkle with garam masala, cilantro, mint, sunflower seeds and cashews, then continue cooking until hot.

TO SERVE: Divide curry among individual bowls.

WINE: Gray Monk Gewurztraminer Reserve has an original Alsace clone showing nutmeg and cinnamon spice.

3 cups chicken stock

5 tsp. grated fresh ginger

5 tsp. minced garlic, mashed to a paste with a bit of salt

1 tsp. chili flakes

1 tsp. turmeric

¾ cup ghee

2 large onions, chopped

2 lbs. chicken breast halves, skinless and boneless, each in 3 pieces

2 tsp. garam masala

⅓ cup chopped fresh cilantro

1 cup chopped fresh mint

2 Tbsp. toasted sunflower seeds

⅓ cup roasted cashew nuts

Aloo Tiki

Aloo Tiki

(Stuffed Potato Cakes)

TRY DRIZZLING these potato cakes with a bit of tamarind chutney before serving. *Serves 6*

POTATO CAKES: Place potatoes in a saucepan and cover with cold water. Bring to a boil on high heat, then turn down the heat to medium-high and cook until fork-tender. Remove from the heat and let cool. Peel potatoes, then grate into a bowl. Stir in cornstarch and salt to taste. Mix well. Divide into 12 portions and roll into balls.

FILLING: Heat oil in a frying pan on medium heat. Add cumin seeds and cook for about 2 minutes, until they begin to crackle. Stir in green peas and cook for 1 minute. Stir in coriander and chili powder, then cook for 1 minute. Remove from the heat and let cool, then mash with a fork. Divide into 12 portions.

FINISH CAKES: Flatten a potato ball in the palm of your hand. Place a portion of the filling on top of it, then gather the edges of the potato ball and pull them over the filling to completely enclose it. Form a ball, then flatten it to make a patty ¾-inch thick. Repeat with the remaining potato balls and filling.

Heat 1 to 2 Tbsp. of the oil in a nonstick frying pan on medium heat. Fry potato patties for 5 minutes per side, until golden and crisp and heated through. (Add more oil, if necessary.) Drain on paper towels.

TO SERVE: Arrange 2 potato cakes on each plate.

WINE: Pair with Gehringer Brothers Estate Winery off-dry Auxerrois or Desert Sun (in the same style blended with Riesling).

POTATO CAKES

2 lbs. Yukon Gold potatoes, unpeeled

4 Tbsp. cornstarch

2 Tbsp. vegetable oil

FILLING

2 Tbsp. vegetable oil

1 tsp. cumin seed

1 cup green peas

2 tsp. coriander powder

1 tsp. chili powder

Duck Breast with Beet and Morel Salad

DUCK

6 duck breast halves,
each 5 oz.

1 tsp. fennel seeds

1 Tbsp. grated fresh ginger

2 Tbsp. chopped fresh mint

⅓ cup canola oil

2 tsp. vegetable oil

SALAD

24 small spring beets,
greens removed

⅓ cup olive oil

1 large leek, white part only,
in 1-inch rounds

24 fresh morel or shiitake
mushrooms, destemmed

¾ cup chicken stock

2 Tbsp. verjus or
1 Tbsp. lemon juice

3 cups baby spinach leaves

Pinch of fleur de sel

VERJUS LITERALLY MEANS "green juice," and it is an acid liquid obtained from unripe grapes. Look for it in specialty gourmet stores. *Serves 6*

DUCK: Use a sharp knife to score duck skin ⅛-inch deep in a cross-hatch pattern. Place in a nonreactive bowl.

Place fennel seeds in a dry saucepan on medium heat and toast for 2 to 3 minutes, until aromatic. Combine fennel seeds, ginger, mint and canola oil in a bowl. Pour over duck, coating all surfaces. Cover bowl with plastic wrap and refrigerate for 24 hours.

Remove duck from the marinade, pat dry with paper towels and place on a plate to come to room temperature. Discard marinade.

SALAD: Place beets in a saucepan and add enough water to cover. Bring to a boil on medium-high heat. Turn down the heat to medium and cook beets for about 20 minutes, until tender. Let cool, then peel and cut into quarters.

Heat oil in a frying pan on medium heat and sauté leeks for 1 to 2 minutes. Add mushrooms and sauté for 1 to 2 minutes. Pour in stock and cook for about 15 minutes, until the mixture is reduced and has the consistency of sauce. Stir in verjus, then remove from the heat. Add beets and let sit at room temperature while the duck is cooking.

FINISH DUCK: Place vegetable oil in a frying pan on medium-high heat. When hot, add duck breasts and sear for 3 to 4 minutes per side, until medium-rare. (The flesh should give slightly when pressed lightly with your fingertip.) Let rest for 5 minutes in a warm place.

FINISH SALAD: Place spinach in large bowl. Use a slotted spoon to transfer beets and morels to the bowl of spinach. Save the pan juices. Toss the salad lightly.

TO SERVE: Divide salad among serving plates. Carve duck into slices about ¼- to ⅓-inch thick and arrange them over the salad. Drizzle with the reserved pan juices and sprinkle with a pinch of fleur de sel.

WINE: A natural match with the Mission Hill Reserve Pinot Noir, with subtle cloves and cherry and raspberry fruit.

{ MISSION HILL FAMILY ESTATE: *michael allemeier* }

Duck Breast with Beet and Morel Salad

Phla Goong

(Prawn Salad)

WILD SALMON, barbecued or cooked under the broiler, is a good substitute for the prawns. *Serves 4*

Bring salted water to a boil in a saucepan on high heat. Add prawns and cook for 2 to 3 minutes, until the shells turn bright pink. Drain, then place under cold running water to stop the cooking. Peel and devein prawns, then place in a large bowl. Add lemon grass, kaffir lime leaves, mint, green onion and cilantro, mixing well. Sprinkle with ground chili pepper and mix.

In a bowl, combine fish sauce, lime juice and sugar. Pour over the prawns and toss lightly.

TO SERVE: Divide salad greens among individual plates, then top with prawn salad.

WINE: Pair with Saturna Island Vineyard's Australia-inspired Semillon Chardonnay.

1 lb. prawns

1 stalk lemon grass, thinly sliced

4 kaffir lime leaves, thinly sliced

¼ cup chopped fresh mint leaves

2 Tbsp. chopped green onion

1 Tbsp. chopped fresh cilantro

¼ tsp. ground dry chili pepper

¼ cup fish sauce

¼ cup lime juice

1 tsp. dark brown sugar

4 cups mixed salad greens
or 8 large red or green leaf
lettuce leaves

Gaeng Keow Wan Gai

(Green Curry Chicken)

¼ cup vegetable oil

2 Tbsp. green curry paste

2 cups coconut milk

1 lb. boneless skinless chicken
breasts, in strips ½ × 2 inches

½ cup fish sauce

2 Tbsp. sugar

2 cups bamboo shoots,
in strips ½ × 2 inches

½ medium to large Japanese
eggplant, in small pieces

1 cup squash, in small pieces

1 cup green beans,
in 1-inch lengths

4 kaffir lime leaves

Small handful of fresh
Thai basil leaves, shredded

1 small red bell pepper,
finely diced, for garnish

SERVE THIS curried chicken with jasmine rice. If you prefer tender rather than crisp green beans, blanch them before adding them to the curry. *Serves 4*

Heat oil in a saucepan on medium heat. Stir in curry paste. Pour in coconut milk and continue stirring until sauce is smooth. Add chicken, fish sauce and sugar, then cook for 2 to 3 minutes. Add bamboo shoots, eggplant, squash, green beans, lime leaves and Thai basil. Cook uncovered (to preserve the green colour of the beans) for 15 minutes, until chicken is just cooked.

TO SERVE: Spoon into individual bowls and garnish with a sprinkle of red bell pepper.

WINE: Sumac Ridge Gewurztraminer Private Reserve off-dry has the spice and light sweetness to marry with the curry.

Khao Neow Dam Piag

(Black Rice Pudding)

COCONUT CREAM is sold in Asian specialty stores, either frozen or in tetra paks. If you cannot find coconut cream, use ½ cup whipping cream lightly whipped with 1 tsp. sugar. *Serves 4 to 6*

PUDDING: Wash rice under running water and discard any chaff or stones. Place rice and water in a heavy saucepan on medium-high heat. Bring to a boil, then turn down the heat to low and simmer for 45 to 50 minutes, stirring occasionally, until rice is soft. Stir in sugar and coconut milk, then cook for 10 minutes.

TOPPING: Mix together coconut cream, sugar and salt in a bowl.

TO SERVE: Serve lukewarm pudding in individual bowls. Garnish with a dollop of coconut cream topping.

WINE: Savour with a glass of St. Hubertus Summer Symphony, an ultra late-harvest Pinot Blanc.

PUDDING

1 cup black Thai rice

6 cups water

½ cup sugar

1 cup coconut milk

TOPPING

½ cup coconut cream

¼ cup sugar

Pinch of salt

Grilled Veal Chops con Queso,

Garlic-roasted Crushed New Potatoes and Arugula Salad

SAUCE

2 cups whipping cream

1 jalapeño pepper, deseeded

1 clove garlic

8 oz. goat cheese, crumbled

POTATOES

1½ lbs. (about 16) new potatoes

1 Tbsp. olive oil

8 cloves garlic, unpeeled

SALAD

2 Tbsp. olive oil or to taste

1 tsp. fresh lemon juice

1 bunch arugula or spinach

VEAL CHOPS

4 veal chops, each 10 to 14 oz.

1 Tbsp. olive oil

MAKE THE CHEESE SAUCE a day ahead and refrigerate it (will keep for 4 days), then reheat it when needed. You can use pork or lamb chops instead of the veal. Remove the chops from the refrigerator half an hour before you plan to cook them.

For a more formal dinner, mound the potatoes in the middle of each plate, arrange the salad on top, then lean a chop on one side. Drizzle 3 to 4 Tbsp. warm cheese sauce around each plate. *Serves 4*

SAUCE: Combine cream, jalapeño pepper, garlic, salt and pepper in a heavy saucepan on medium heat. Bring to a simmer and cook for 10 minutes. Remove from the heat, then slowly add goat cheese, mixing with a hand-held blender until smooth. Keep warm.

POTATOES: Preheat the oven to 375°F. Place potatoes, oil, garlic and a pinch of salt and pepper in a roasting pan, then toss to coat potatoes evenly. Roast in the oven for 20 to 25 minutes, or until easily pierced with a fork.

Remove from the oven, then peel garlic and discard the skins. Crush potatoes and garlic gently with the back of a fork. (Add 1 or 2 tsp. olive oil if the mixture seems too dry.) Cover with aluminum foil to keep warm.

SALAD: Whisk together oil, lemon juice and a pinch of salt and pepper in a bowl. Place arugula in a salad bowl, pour in dressing, then toss lightly.

VEAL CHOPS: Preheat the barbecue or broiler to high. Brush veal chops with oil, then season with salt and pepper. Grill for 4 to 8 minutes per side, until medium-rare (the meat will be pink in the centre). For medium or well-done, cook a little longer.

TO SERVE: Divide the salad among individual plates. Arrange a veal chop and some crushed potatoes beside the salad. Drizzle veal with warm cheese sauce.

WINE: A big, oaky rich Chardonnay pairs well with the veal—try a glass of Township 7—or an elegant red.

Grilled Veal Chops con Queso, Garlic-roasted Crushed New Potatoes and Arugula Salad

Chai Crème Brûlée

GARNISH THIS DESSERT with some fresh berries and serve with a few crisp cookies. *Serves 6*

Preheat the oven to 350°F. Set out six 1-cup ceramic ramekins.

Place egg yolks and the ¾ cup of sugar in the bowl of an electric mixer. Beat on high speed for about 5 minutes, until the mixture forms a ribbon when the beaters are lifted. Transfer to a bowl.

Place creamo, whipping cream and tea bags in a heavy saucepan on medium heat. Bring to a boil, then remove from the heat and discard the tea bags.

Slowly whisk a little of the cream mixture into the egg mixture. Use a wooden spoon to gently stir in the remaining cream mixture. Continue to stir until the custard is completely blended. (Do not whisk, or you will incorporate too much air and the custard will not be thick and velvety.)

Divide the custard among the ramekins. Set the ramekins in a large roasting pan and add enough hot water to reach halfway up the sides of the dishes. Bake in the oven for 35 to 45 minutes. Gently shake the ramekins, and if the custard jiggles slightly, it is done. Remove the ramekins from the roasting pan and let cool, then refrigerate overnight.

TO SERVE: Preheat the broiler to high. Evenly sprinkle 1 Tbsp. of sugar over each ramekin. Place them under the broiler, or heat the tops with a propane blowtorch, until sugar is bubbling and caramelized. Watch carefully so that they do not burn. Set each ramekin on a plate and serve.

WINE: Sip an Ehrenfelser Select Late Harvest with hints of green tea, from Calona Vineyard's Private Reserve.

10 egg yolks

¾ cup sugar + 6 Tbsp. for caramelizing

2 cups creamo or half and half cream

2 cups whipping cream

2 or 3 chai tea bags or any other tea bags

{ **PAPRIKA BISTRO**: *george szasz* }

Veal Goulash over Hungarian Spaetzle with Lecso

Veal Goulash over Hungarian Spaetzle with Lecso

IN HUNGARY, *spaetzle,* or noodles, are known as *galuska.* They are a traditional accompaniment to goulash. *Lecso* is a vegetable dish made from tomatoes and green peppers. *Serves 4*

SPAETZLE: Place a large saucepan two thirds full of water on high heat. Cover with a lid and bring to a boil, then turn down the heat to medium-low so the water remains at a gentle boil.

Combine flour, salt, eggs and milk in a large bowl. Mix until the dough resembles a soft muffin batter. Do not overbeat. Press the dough, a bit at a time, through a perforated pizza pan or a spaetzle maker so that the strips fall directly into the boiling water. Cook for 5 to 8 minutes, until they rise to the surface. Use a slotted spoon to transfer spaetzle to a plate or drain in a colander. Keep warm.

GOULASH: Heat oil in a frying pan on medium-high heat. Sauté onion for 5 minutes, until it begins to brown. Stir in green pepper and tomatoes, turn down the heat to medium-low and cook for 5 minutes, until vegetables are soft. Stir in paprika, caraway, salt and pepper. Add veal and simmer, partly covered, for 90 minutes, until the meat melts in your mouth. Lower the heat, if necessary, so that the mixture bubbles gently.

LECSO: Fry bacon in a saucepan on medium-low heat for 3 to 4 minutes, until it renders its fat. Add the additional fat, then sauté onion for about 15 minutes, until transparent. Stir in peppers, tomatoes, paprika and salt. Cover with a lid and simmer gently, stirring occasionally, for 20 minutes. Add smoked sausage (optional) and cook for 10 minutes, until peppers are tender and the ingredients are heated through.

TO SERVE: Divide the spaetzle among individual plates. Top with goulash and a dollop of sour cream. Add several spoonfuls of lecso on the side.

WINE: Try Mt. Boucherie Estate Winery Blaufrankisch (Lemberger) Summit Reserve with its nutmeg and spearmint, or Benchland Vineyard's spicy Zweigelt showing fennel and sage.

SPAETZLE

3 cups all-purpose flour

1½ tsp. salt

4 eggs

½ cup whole milk

GOULASH

3 Tbsp. vegetable oil
(not olive oil)

1 onion, diced

1 green pepper,
deseeded and diced

3 tomatoes, peeled and diced
or 2 cups drained chopped
canned tomatoes

3 tsp. Hungarian paprika

1 tsp. ground caraway seed
(use a spice mill to grind)

1 tsp. salt

¼ tsp. black pepper

2 lbs. veal shoulder or boneless
shank, in 1-inch cubes

4 Tbsp. sour cream for garnish

LECSO

⅓ cup bacon, diced

2 Tbsp. bacon fat

1 onion, diced

1 lb. mixed green peppers
and Hungarian wax peppers,
deseeded, in lengthwise
½-inch slices

1 lb. tomatoes,
deseeded and quartered

1 tsp. Hungarian paprika

1 tsp. salt

8 oz. smoked sausage
(optional)

Roast Breast of Squab

with Braised Lentils, and Sherry Vinegar and White Truffle–Honey Sauce

LENTILS

4 cups water

1 cup Puy lentils

4 Tbsp. extra-virgin olive oil

1 clove garlic, minced

1 small onion, in small dice

1 small carrot, in small dice

1 rib celery, in small dice

2 slices smoked bacon,
in small dice

4 fresh basil leaves, shredded

½ tsp. fennel seeds

½ cup drained and chopped
canned plum tomatoes

½ cup chicken stock

Olive oil for garnish

SQUAB

2 squabs, each 14 to 16 oz.

1 cup all-purpose flour

1 Tbsp. butter

2 Tbsp. vegetable oil

SAUCE

1 cup chicken stock

½ cup medium-dry sherry

½ cup sherry vinegar

4 Tbsp. unpasteurized honey

2 Tbsp. unsalted butter

2 tsp. white truffle oil

2 sprigs fresh thyme, leaves only

SQUAB is a rich dark meat that is best served medium-rare. Be sure to cook the lentils in unsalted water, as salt will make the lentils tough. *Serves 4*

LENTILS: Bring water to a boil in a saucepan on high heat. Add lentils, turn down the heat to low, then cook for 20 minutes, until just tender. Drain and let cool. Do not rinse the cooked lentils.

Heat oil in a frying pan on medium heat. Sauté garlic, onion, carrot, celery, bacon, basil and fennel seeds for about 2 minutes, until vegetables begin to soften. Stir in lentils and tomatoes, then pour in stock and cook until the mixture becomes the consistency of a dense stew. Season with salt and pepper. Remove from the heat and keep warm.

SQUAB: Preheat the oven to 450°F. Remove the breasts from squabs and save the legs and carcasses for another use. Season breasts with salt and pepper.

Pour flour onto a shallow dish. Press squab breasts, skin side down, into flour, then gently shake off any excess.

Heat butter and oil in a heavy ovenproof frying pan on medium-high heat for 1 to 2 minutes, until it begins to turn golden. Add squab, skin side down, and sauté for 1 minute. Place the pan in the oven and roast for 4 to 5 minutes, until squab is tender and pink. Do not overcook. Remove the pan from the oven, turn over the squab, then let sit for 1 minute. Transfer to a warm platter.

SAUCE: Place stock in a saucepan on medium-high heat and cook for 4 to 5 minutes, until reduced to half. Stir in sherry and vinegar, then cook for about 3 minutes, until reduced to half. Stir in honey, then boil the sauce until it becomes loose and syrupy. Remove from the heat, then whisk in butter, white truffle oil and thyme. Season with salt and pepper.

TO SERVE: Divide lentils among individual plates and garnish with a small splash of olive oil. Slice each half breast into 3 pieces and arrange over the lentils. Spoon some sauce around each plate.

WINE: Blue Mountain Pinot Noir has the Burgundian style and balance to suit small game birds.

Roast Breast of Squab with Braised Lentils, and Sherry Vinegar and White Truffle–Honey Sauce

Pork Tenderloin Schnitzel

with Crème Fraîche Mustard Sauce

CRÈME FRAÎCHE

1 cup whipping cream

⅓ cup buttermilk

SAUCE

1 cup chicken stock

2 shallots, finely minced

1 cup crème fraîche or
whipping cream

2 Tbsp. Dijon mustard,
preferably extra strong

1 Tbsp. grainy mustard

¼ cup chopped fresh parsley

PORK

1 lb. pork tenderloin,
in 8 equal pieces

1 cup flour

1 cup dry bread crumbs

3 eggs

½ cup vegetable oil

2 Tbsp. butter

BEGIN PREPARING the crème fraîche a few days before you plan to serve this dish. Crème fraîche will keep, refrigerated, for up to 10 days.

At Parkside, we serve the schnitzel garnished with choucroute (sauerkraut) and mustard sauce, but you could substitute a few wedges of lemon and some boiled potatoes tossed with parsley and butter. *Serves 4*

CRÈME FRAÎCHE: Mix together cream and buttermilk in a non-reactive container. Cover tightly with plastic wrap and let sit in a warm place for 48 to 72 hours, until slightly thickened.

SAUCE: Place stock and shallots in a saucepan on medium-high heat. Bring to a boil and cook for about 10 minutes, until reduced to one quarter. Add crème fraîche and bring to a boil, then turn down the heat to medium-low and simmer for 8 to 10 minutes, until reduced to about ½ cup. Whisk in Dijon and grainy mustards until sauce is smooth. Stir in parsley just before serving.

PORK: Place pork between two sheets of plastic wrap. Use a mallet or a rolling pin to pound pork until it is about ¼-inch thick. Season with salt and pepper.

Place flour and bread crumbs on separate plates. Place eggs in a shallow bowl and beat. Dredge each piece of pork in flour, dip it into egg and coat well with bread crumbs.

Heat oil and butter in a heavy frying pan on medium heat. To test the oil temperature, drop a small piece of bread into the hot oil. If it turns golden in 30 seconds or so, the temperature is correct. If it darkens too quickly, reduce the heat and wait for 1 minute before adding the pork. (Be careful not to overheat the oil, or the coating will brown before the meat is cooked.) Fry pork in batches, for about 4 minutes per side, until golden brown. Keep warm in a low oven while the next batch is frying.

TO SERVE: Arrange 2 pork schnitzels on each plate, then spoon sauce around them.

WINE: A nice match is the ripe, round Merlot from Calona Vineyard's Artist Series.

Crab Bisque

HE STRAINED STOCK can be frozen for up to 2 months. Thaw it overnight in the refrigerator, then heat it, add the whipping cream and reduce.

Foaming the bisque makes for a more formal presentation and a thicker, more luxurious-tasting soup. We use a nitrous foamer at the restaurant, but a hand-held blender or a battery-powered foamer also works well. *Serves 6 to 8*

Preheat the oven to 300°F. Remove crabmeat from the body, claws and larger legs. Save for use in another recipe or to garnish the bisque. Roughly chop the shell and small legs.

Heat oil in an ovenproof saucepan on medium heat. Add the chopped crab shells and cook for 5 to 8 minutes. Stir in onion, celery, carrot and garlic, then cook for 10 minutes. Stir in tomato paste. Place the saucepan in the oven and bake for about 20 minutes, until tomato paste glazes the crab shells and vegetables.

Remove the saucepan from the oven and place it on the stove on medium-high heat. Add vermouth and deglaze. Cook for 3 to 4 minutes, until the sauce is reduced and most of the liquid has evaporated. Add stock and bay leaf, then bring to a boil. Skim off and discard scum. Turn down the heat to low and simmer for about 30 minutes.

Strain the stock through a fine-mesh sieve into a clean pot and discard any solids. Cook on medium heat for about 20 to 30 minutes, until reduced to one third. Stir in cream and cook for 15 minutes, until reduced to one third. Strain the bisque through a fine-mesh sieve and discard any solids.

TO SERVE: Froth the bisque, then pour it into small soup bowls or demitasse cups.

WINE: CedarCreek's crisper Chardonnay or its richer Platinum Reserve Chardonnay both see French oak, resulting in complex creaminess.

1 crab, 1½ to 2 lbs., cooked
3 Tbsp. olive oil
1 onion, diced
1 rib celery, diced
1 carrot, diced
1 clove garlic, crushed
1 tsp. tomato paste
⅓ cup white vermouth
12 cups chicken stock
1 bay leaf
1 cup whipping cream

Crab Bisque

Squab Breast and Confit Legs

with Mustard Sabayon

SAVE THE DUCK FAT in which you cook the squab legs. Strain it through a fine-mesh sieve and refrigerate; will keep for up to 2 weeks. Use it to sauté potatoes.

If you are short on time, cook only the squab breasts. Save the legs and use them to make stock. *Serves 4*

SQUAB: Cut off the legs. Detach the breasts but leave them on the bone. Refrigerate the breasts, covered, until needed. Remove the backbone and save it for making chicken stock.

Combine salt and pepper, then rub into the squab legs. Place the legs in a bowl, cover and refrigerate for 3 hours.

Preheat the oven to 175°F. Wipe squab legs with paper towels to remove the salt and pepper. Place legs in a baking dish just large enough to hold them in a single layer. Completely cover the legs with melted duck fat. Cover with a lid, then cook in the oven for 3 hours. Remove from the oven and let cool in the pan.

Turn up the oven to 475°F. Rub squab breasts with oil, then season with salt and pepper. Heat a nonstick frying pan on medium-high heat. Sear squab breasts, skin side down, for 1 to 2 minutes. Place them, skin side up, on a baking sheet and roast in the oven for 10 minutes. Brush the skin with honey, then roast for 2 minutes, until the skin is glazed. Remove from the oven and let rest for 5 minutes. Turn down the oven to 325°F.

SABAYON: Place all the ingredients in a stainless steel bowl. Season with salt and pepper. Place the bowl over a saucepan of simmering but not boiling water on low heat. Whisk constantly, being careful not to scramble the eggs, for 8 to 10 minutes, until tripled in volume. Remove from the heat.

FINISH SQUAB: Return squab breasts to the oven and reheat for 3 to 4 minutes. Cut breast halves away from the bone.

Wipe off excess fat from squab legs with paper towels. Heat a nonstick frying pan on high heat and sauté the legs until crisp, about 1 to 2 minutes.

TO SERVE: Place a breast half and a leg on each plate. Spoon mustard sabayon beside the meat.

WINE: Blue Mountain Pinot Noir Reserve "Stripe Label."

SQUAB

2 squabs, each 14 to 16 oz.

2 Tbsp. salt

¾ tsp. freshly ground black pepper

3½ to 4 cups duck fat, melted, or olive oil

1 tsp. vegetable oil

2 Tbsp. liquid honey

SABAYON

2 egg yolks

1 egg

1 Tbsp. Dijon mustard

3 Tbsp. Sauvignon Blanc or other dry white wine

1 tsp. lemon juice

2 Tbsp. white vermouth

Hot and Sour Soup

2½ cups chicken stock

2 Tbsp. tamarind paste

1 tsp. salt

2 Tbsp. sugar

1 Tbsp. fish sauce

3 fresh Thai chilies, chopped

3½ oz. fresh prawns, peeled

2 tomatoes, chopped

¼ fresh pineapple or
½ 14 oz. can, chopped

2 Tbsp. vegetable oil

4 cloves garlic, chopped

2 to 3 Tbsp. fresh basil, chopped

THIS CAMBODIAN/VIETNAMESE version of hot and sour soup is intensely flavoured and studded with fresh prawns. *Serves 4*

Place stock, tamarind, salt, sugar, fish sauce and chilies in a saucepan on medium-high heat. Bring to a boil and cook for 7 minutes. Strain through a fine-mesh sieve into a clean saucepan and discard the solids. Add prawns, tomatoes and pineapple, then cook for 8 minutes, until prawns are opaque and pink in colour.

While the prawns are cooking, heat oil in a frying pan on medium heat. Sauté garlic for about 3 minutes, until golden brown.

TO SERVE: Pour soup into individual bowls. Garnish with garlic and basil.

WINE: A refreshing Granville Island lager; a Bowen Island smooth, hoppy bitter, or a Bear Brewing porter-style Black Bear ale—all are good choices.

{ PHNOM PENH: *peter huynh* }

Hot and Sour Soup

Ga Xe Phai

(Chicken Salad)

SALAD

1 lb. (½ large or 1 small head)
cabbage, shredded

1 carrot, shredded

1 chicken breast, about 6 oz.

1 chicken thigh, 4 to 5 oz.

2 to 3 Tbsp. fresh basil
for garnish

2 to 3 Tbsp. fresh
rau ram for garnish

½ cup chopped salted peanuts
for garnish (optional)

DRESSING

3 Tbsp. sugar

2 Tbsp. fish sauce

2 Tbsp. Vietnamese
garlic-chili sauce

1 small lime, juice of

RAU RAM is Vietnamese coriander. It is available from Asian specialty stores, but if you cannot find it, use fresh cilantro. *Serves 6*

SALAD: Place cabbage and carrot in a large bowl, cover with cold water and place in the refrigerator to soak for 30 minutes. Drain well and spin dry. Transfer to a serving bowl.

Place 2 cups of water in a saucepan on high heat. Bring to a boil, then add chicken breast and thigh. Reduce heat to medium-low, then simmer for 15 to 20 minutes, until just cooked. Use a slotted spoon to remove chicken from the water. Rinse under cold running water, then pat dry with paper towels. Remove and discard skin and bones. Roughly tear chicken meat into long strips and place on top of the vegetables.

DRESSING: Combine sugar, fish sauce, garlic-chili sauce, lime juice and 2 Tbsp. of water in a bowl.

TO SERVE: Drizzle the dressing over the vegetables and chicken. Garnish with basil, rau ram and peanuts (optional).

WINE: Try a fresh crisp Riesling such as the one from Gehringer Brothers Private Reserve, which has hints of nectarine and peaches.

Zuppa di Pesce
(Fish Soup)

USE A COMBINATION of different types of fish to make this soup. One good combination is halibut, turbot, rock cod and red snapper. Serve this soup with garlic croutons and saffron mayonnaise. *Serves 4*

Place all of the ingredients in a stockpot and add enough cold water to cover. Bring to a boil on medium-high heat, then turn down the heat to medium-low and cook for 2 hours until reduced by one third. Remove soup from the heat and let cool for 10 to 15 minutes.

Pass soup through a food mill or pulse in a food processor to achieve a rough purée. Strain through a wide-mesh sieve into a clean saucepan. Season with salt and pepper.

TO SERVE: Reheat soup gently on low heat and pour into a tureen or individual bowls.

WINE: Match with the creamy and spicy Township 7 Seven Stars Sparkling with extended tirage.

2¼ lbs. white-fleshed fish, scaled, gutted, in chunks

1 onion, chopped

2 ribs celery, chopped

1 leek, chopped

5 cloves garlic, crushed

1½ cups chopped tomatoes, peeled and deseeded

1 sprig thyme

1 bulb fennel, chopped

Pinch of saffron

3 Tbsp. + 2 tsp. olive oil

1 strip of orange peel

1 bay leaf

½ tsp. salt

{ **PICCOLO MONDO RISTORANTE:** *stephane meyer* }

Ravioli alle Melanzane

Ravioli alle Melanzane

(Eggplant Ravioli)

EGGPLANT, *melanzane* to Italians, makes a creamy, satisfying filling for pasta. *Serves 6*

FILLING: Preheat the oven to 350°F. Cut eggplant in half lengthwise, then score the flesh ½-inch deep in a cross-hatch pattern.

Combine garlic, thyme, 1 Tbsp. of the oil, salt and pepper in a bowl, then rub into eggplant. Place the eggplant on a cookie sheet and bake in the oven for 45 minutes, until the flesh is soft. Remove from the oven and let cool enough to handle easily. Peel eggplant and chop the flesh. Place in a bowl and toss with the remaining oil and chervil. Season with salt and pepper.

RAVIOLI: Line a cookie sheet with parchment paper.

Divide dough into 4 portions. Roll out each portion to a rectangle 16 × 4 inches with a thickness of ⅛ inch or thinner, if possible. Lay a sheet of dough on a lightly floured work surface. Place 1 Tbsp. of filling at 2-inch intervals, until you have 32 pieces.

Fill a cup with water. Dip your finger in the water and trace a square around each of the filling mounds.

Place the second sheet of dough over the first. Press firmly around each of the filling mounds to seal the ravioli. Use a sharp knife to cut the pasta into 32 squares, or use a round fluted cookie cutter 1¾ inches in diameter. Press down around edges to seal.

Bring a stockpot of salted water to a boil on high heat. Drop the ravioli into the boiling water in batches. Cook for 4 minutes, until pasta is al dente. Use a slotted spoon to transfer pasta to the cookie sheet.

SAUCE: Place stock in a saucepan (large enough to hold the ravioli) and bring to a boil on medium-high heat. Add tomato. Stir in butter and oil, season with salt and pepper, then cook for 1 minute. Add the cooked ravioli and turn down the heat to medium-low, then cook for 2 to 3 minutes, until warmed through. Season with salt and pepper.

TO SERVE: Transfer to a serving bowl or arrange on individual plates. Garnish with chervil.

WINE: Pair with the rich but balanced Blue Mountain Chardonnay (or the bigger Reserve "Stripe Label").

FILLING

1 eggplant

1 clove garlic, chopped

1 tsp. chopped fresh thyme,

3 Tbsp. olive oil

2 Tbsp. chopped fresh chervil

RAVIOLI

1 lb. fresh pasta dough (page 151), omit the saffron, or 6 fresh lasagne sheets or 64 won ton wrappers

SAUCE

¾ cup chicken stock

1 small to medium tomato, peeled, deseeded, in small dice

1½ tsp. butter

3 Tbsp. olive oil

6 fresh chervil sprigs for garnish

Baccala Gratinato con Pinoli e Sultanina

(Baked Salt Cod with Pine Nuts and Raisins)

FISH

1 lb. salt cod

1 cup milk

4 Tbsp. butter

1 onion, finely chopped

2/3 cup whipping cream

2 Tbsp. Parmesan cheese,
freshly grated

SAUCE

1/2 cup fish stock

1/2 cup whipping cream

1 Tbsp. raisins

1 Tbsp. toasted pine nuts

SOME SALT COD is much saltier than others and can take up to 3 days to soak. Test a small piece after 1 day; you want a pleasant salty taste that is not overwhelming. If it is still too salty, continue soaking the fish in water, changing the water a few times a day.

Serve this dish with crusty bread and a simple green salad.
Serves 6 as a starter, or 4 as a main course

FISH: Place salt cod in a bowl, add enough cold water to cover and refrigerate overnight. Drain and discard the water. Add enough cold water to cover and refrigerate for another 4 hours. Drain well, then break fish into small pieces.

Preheat the oven to 300°F.

Place milk in a saucepan on medium heat. Add fish and cook for 10 minutes, until mushy.

Melt butter in another saucepan on medium heat and sauté onions for 15 minutes, until translucent. Stir in cream and cook for 15 minutes. Add fish and Parmesan. Turn down the heat to low and cook for about 20 minutes, until the mixture has the consistency of mashed potatoes. Season with freshly ground black pepper.

Transfer the mixture to a 6-cup baking dish and bake in the oven for 15 to 20 minutes, until the top is crusty.

SAUCE: Place stock in a saucepan on medium-high heat and bring to a boil. Stir in cream and simmer for 10 minutes. Add raisins and pine nuts, then cook for 5 minutes. Season with salt and pepper.

TO SERVE: Divide the fish mixture among 4 to 6 warm shallow bowls. Top with the sauce.

WINE: Creamy and spicy Tinhorn Creek Chardonnay is a lovely match for bacalao.

Vancouver Island Asparagus and Yukon Gold Potato Purée

with Spot Prawn and Butternut Squash Custard

THIS SURPRISING CUSTARD is surrounded by a delicately flavoured purée, an excellent start for any springtime meal. *Serves 4*

POTATO PURÉE: Heat oil in a heavy saucepan on medium heat. Add garlic and onion, then turn down the heat to low. Cover with a lid and cook for 3 to 5 minutes, until onion is soft. Add potato and cook for 2 to 3 minutes. Add stock and cook for about 5 minutes, until potatoes are done. Add asparagus and cook for 3 to 4 minutes, until tender. Remove from the heat and let cool for 10 minutes.

Transfer to a blender. Add spinach, then purée on high speed. Strain through a fine-mesh sieve into a clean saucepan. Season with salt and pepper.

CUSTARD: Preheat the oven to 325°F. Grease four ½-cup ramekins. Line the bottom of each ramekin with parchment paper, then butter the paper.

Whisk together eggs and cream in a bowl. Stir in nutmeg. Season with salt and pepper.

Divide prawns, squash and chives among the ramekins. Fill each ramekin three quarters full with the egg mixture. Set the ramekins in a large roasting pan and add enough water to reach halfway up the sides of the dishes. Bake in the oven for about 25 minutes. Gently shake the ramekins, and if the custard jiggles slightly, it is done. Remove from the oven and take the ramekins out of the roasting pan. Let cool slightly.

TO SERVE: Reheat potato purée and spoon into shallow soup bowls.

Run a knife around the edge of each custard. Place a plate over the top of each ramekin, then invert both ramekin and the plate at the same time. Unmould the custard, then remove the parchment paper. Place a custard on top of each serving of potato purée.

WINE: Savour the dry Cuvée de Pinot, which combines mostly Gris with Blanc and Auxerrois, from Cherry Point Vineyards in Cobble Hill, on Vancouver Island.

POTATO PURÉE

1 Tbsp. vegetable oil

1 clove elephant garlic, minced

½ white onion, in small dice

1 large Yukon Gold potato, peeled and in small dice

6 cups vegetable stock

1½ lbs. asparagus, trimmed and chopped

2 handfuls spinach leaves

CUSTARD

3 large eggs

1 cup whipping cream

Pinch of nutmeg

6 to 8 spot prawns, peeled, deveined and chopped

1 cup butternut squash, peeled, blanched, in very small dice

2 Tbsp. finely chopped fresh chives

{ POINTE RESTAURANT AT THE WICKANINNISH INN: *andrew springett* }

Vancouver Island Asparagus and Yukon Gold Potato Purée with Spot Prawn and Butternut Squash Custard

Sun-dried Tomato and Pancetta–stuffed Chicken Breast

with Yam, Celeriac and Red Onion Hash in Fresh Sage-Fennel Cream Sauce

THESE COOKED stuffed chicken breasts make a delicious summer meal when sliced and served cold with a green salad and some crispy bread. *Serves 4*

CHICKEN: Preheat the oven to 375°F.

To make the stuffing, trim chicken breasts to 5½ to 6 oz. Reserve the flesh from these trimmings but discard the trimmed skin. Place chicken trimmings, sun-dried tomatoes, pancetta and cream in a food processor. Blend until smooth, then transfer to a bowl.

Use a finger to draw back the skin from a chicken breast. Spread the stuffing between the skin and the flesh as evenly as possible. Season chicken with salt and pepper.

Heat oil in an ovenproof frying pan on medium-high heat. Sear chicken, skin side down, for 3 to 5 minutes, until golden brown. Turn chicken over, then roast in the oven for about 15 minutes, until a meat thermometer reads 165°F. Remove from the oven and let rest for about 5 minutes before carving. Slice each chicken breast half into 5 pieces.

While the chicken is roasting, prepare the hash and the sauce.

HASH: Heat oil in a saucepan on medium heat. Sauté yams, celeriac and onion for 10 to 15 minutes, until slightly caramelized. Season with salt and pepper. Keep warm.

SAUCE: Heat oil in a saucepan on medium-high heat. Sauté onion, garlic and fennel for about 10 minutes, until tender. Add wine and deglaze the saucepan, then cook for about 5 minutes, until reduced to half. Stir in stock and cook for about 10 minutes, until reduced to half. Stir in cream and cook for about 5 minutes, until the sauce coats the back of a spoon. Remove from the heat and let cool for 10 minutes. *continued overleaf >*

CHICKEN

4 boneless chicken breast halves, skin on, each 6 to 8 oz.

2 Tbsp. rehydrated and julienned sun-dried tomatoes

4 oz. pancetta, baked until crisp

2 Tbsp. whipping cream

1 Tbsp. vegetable oil

HASH

2 tsp. vegetable oil

1 cup small dice yams

1 cup small dice celeriac

¼ cup julienned red onion

SAUCE

2 tsp. vegetable oil

½ white onion, in small dice

1 clove elephant garlic, minced

½ bulb fennel

1¼ cups Chardonnay or other dry white wine

1¼ cups vegetable stock

1⅓ cups whipping cream

2 Tbsp. chopped fresh sage leaves

Purée in a blender until smooth. Strain through a fine-mesh sieve into a clean saucepan. Reheat on medium-low heat for about 5 minutes. Season with salt and pepper, then stir in sage.

TO SERVE: Spoon hash into the middle of each plate. Arrange chicken slices in a fan shape on top of the hash. Drizzle a little sauce around the edge, then serve the remainder in a sauce-boat on the side.

WINE: Try Calliope's Merlot: the softer American-oaked one with a dash of Cabernet Sauvignon from Rock Rose Vineyard in Osoyoos, or the more concentrated 100% Merlot from Oak Knoll Vineyard in Kaleden.

Roasted Roma Tomato Soup

ROASTING THE TOMATOES gives this soup additional flavour and colour. *Serves 4*

SOUP: Preheat the oven to 400°F.

Place tomatoes, cut side up, on a large cookie sheet. Drizzle with oil, then sprinkle with herbes de Provence, ¼ tsp. of the salt and the pepper. Bake in the oven for 1 hour, until tomatoes are soft and wrinkled. Check tomatoes occasionally while they are cooking to make sure they do not burn (turn down the heat, if necessary).

Place roasted tomatoes, their pan juices, water, garlic and the remaining salt in a saucepan on medium heat. Bring to a boil, then turn down the heat and simmer for 30 minutes. Strain through a fine-mesh sieve into a clean bowl, pressing the solids with a wooden spoon. Discard the solids. Season with salt and pepper.

CROUTONS: Preheat the oven to 350°F. Place bread cubes in a bowl.

Combine butter, red pepper flakes, garlic and parsley in a saucepan on medium heat. Cook, stirring constantly, for about 3 minutes, until bubbling. Pour over bread cubes and toss to coat evenly.

Spread out bread cubes on a cookie sheet and bake in the oven for about 8 minutes, until lightly golden. Remove from the oven and drain on paper towels.

TO SERVE: Reheat the soup and ladle into individual bowls. Sprinkle with croutons, garnish with basil and drizzle with oil.

WINE: Domaine Combret Rosé from Cabernet Franc grapes has a light red tomato colour and clean crisp tangerine acidity.

SOUP

2½ lbs. (about 15) Roma tomatoes, halved lengthwise

⅓ cup extra-virgin olive oil

2 Tbsp. herbes de Provence

½ tsp. salt

¼ tsp. freshly ground black pepper

4 cups water

1 bulb garlic, separated into cloves and peeled

6 finely sliced fresh basil leaves for garnish

Extra-virgin olive oil for garnish

CROUTONS

1 cup cubed French baguette, each ⅓ inch

3 Tbsp. butter

½ tsp. hot red pepper flakes

1 Tbsp. minced garlic

2 tsp. chopped fresh parsley

Grilled Halibut

with Spring Asparagus, Saffron New Potatoes and Olive Tapenade

TAPENADE

1¼ cups pitted black olives
(preferably kalamata
or niçoise)

4 Tbsp. drained and
rinsed capers

8 fillets anchovy

5 cloves garlic

1 cup + 2 tsp. extra-virgin
olive oil

POTATOES

4 cups water

2 pinches saffron

8 new potatoes,
in ½-inch slices

ASPARAGUS

20 large stalks
asparagus, trimmed

1 Tbsp. olive oil

HALIBUT

4 fillets of halibut, each 6 oz.

2 Tbsp. olive oil

To save time, cook the potatoes until tender in advance and reheat them just before serving. The tapenade will keep for up to 2 weeks in the refrigerator. Serve any leftover tapenade on croutons as an appetizer.

If you do not have a barbecue, blanch the asparagus in a pot of boiling salted water for 4 to 5 minutes, until tender and green. Plunge them in ice water to stop the cooking. The fish can be grilled in the oven for 8 minutes. Rub the grill pan with canola oil to prevent the fish from sticking. *Serves 4*

TAPENADE: Place olives, capers, anchovies, garlic and 1 cup of oil in a food processor. Process until smooth. Transfer to a bowl, cover and refrigerate until needed.

POTATOES: Place water in a saucepan, add saffron and let infuse for 30 minutes. Turn on the heat to medium-high and bring water to a simmer. Add potatoes and cook for 5 to 8 minutes, until just soft but not breaking apart. Drain, place in a bowl and keep warm.

ASPARAGUS: Preheat the barbecue to medium-high. Drizzle asparagus with oil, then season with salt and pepper. Grill on the barbecue for about 10 minutes, turning from time to time, until tender. Keep warm. Leave the barbecue on.

HALIBUT: Rub halibut with oil, then season with salt and pepper. Grill on the barbecue, with the lid down, for 6 to 8 minutes, until flesh is opaque. (The fish will continue to cook off the heat, so be careful not to overcook it.) Transfer to a clean plate.

FINISH TAPENADE: Combine ¼ cup of the tapenade with the 1 to 2 tsp. of oil.

TO SERVE: Place 5 stalks of asparagus on each plate. Arrange potatoes across the bottom half of the asparagus. Top with a piece of halibut. Drizzle tapenade evenly over and around each plate.

WINE: Sumac Ridge Chardonnay from Black Sage Vineyard is round with full tropical fruit.

{ PROVENCE MEDITERRANEAN GRILL AND PROVENCE MARINASIDE:

alessandra & jean-francis quaglia }

Grilled Halibut with Spring Asparagus, Saffron New Potatoes and Olive Tapenade

Lemon Tarts

PASTRY

2 cups all-purpose flour

⅓ cup sugar

⅓ lb. cold butter, cubed

1 egg, lightly beaten

1 to 2 Tbsp. ice water

FILLING

1 cup fresh lemon juice
(8 or 9 lemons)

3 lemons, zest of

2½ cups cold water

6 eggs

¾ cup sugar

1 tsp. vanilla

½ cup cornstarch

FOR A MORE festive dessert, serve these tarts with hazelnut brittle, whipped cream and fruit coulis. *Serves 6*

PASTRY: Combine flour and sugar in a bowl. Use a pastry blender or two knives to cut in butter until the mixture is the size of small peas. Make a well in the middle and add egg. Stir lightly with a fork, adding enough of the ice water to allow the dough to adhere to itself when pressed. Gather the dough into a ball, then flatten it into a disk. Wrap the dough in plastic wrap and refrigerate for at least 30 minutes.

Lightly flour a work surface. Roll out the dough to a thickness of ⅛ inch. Cut out 6 circles, each about 5 inches in diameter (or the size to fit your tart pans). Line the tart pans with dough, then refrigerate them for 30 minutes.

Preheat the oven to 375°F. Line the tart pans with aluminum foil, then fill them with pie weights or dried beans. Bake in the oven for 15 to 20 minutes, until pale golden brown. Remove from the oven and turn down the oven temperature to 350°F. Take out the pie weights and the aluminum foil, then cool tart shells on a wire rack.

FILLING: Combine all the ingredients in a saucepan on medium heat. Use a wooden spoon to stir constantly and cook for about 8 to 10 minutes, until the mixture becomes thick and begins to bubble. Remove from the heat and let cool slightly.

Pour the filling into the tart shells. Bake in the oven for 10 to 15 minutes, until the filling is set. Let cool, then refrigerate for 2 to 3 hours, until filling is set.

TO SERVE: Unmould the tarts and place them on individual plates.

WINE: Sip a glass of off-dry Amy's Riesling, with refreshing green apple and tropical lime, from Scherzinger Vineyards in Summerland.

Buffalo Mozzarella with Hazelnut and Arugula Crostini

START THIS SALAD the day before you plan to serve it, so that the mozzarella can marinate overnight. *Serves 4*

Place mozzarella and oil in a bowl. Cover with plastic wrap and marinate overnight in the refrigerator. Use a slotted spoon to transfer mozzarella to a clean bowl. Reserve the oil.

Preheat the broiler. Arrange baguette slices on a cookie sheet and drizzle with the reserved olive oil. Sprinkle with ground hazelnuts and broil for about 2 minutes, until golden brown. Remove from the broiler but leave the broiler on.

Sprinkle the baguette slices with arugula and top with mozzarella. Sprinkle with Parmigiano-Reggiano. Return to the broiler for about 30 seconds, until the cheese melts slightly.

TO SERVE: Arrange the crostini on a serving platter or divide among individual plates.

WINE: Pair with Sumac Ridge Blanc de Noirs from Pinot Noir grapes instead of an Italian Prosecco.

14 oz. buffalo mozzarella, in ½-inch cubes

2 Tbsp. extra-virgin olive oil

1 baguette, in ½-inch slices

4 oz. ground roasted hazelnuts

24 arugula leaves, in chiffonade

2 oz. Parmigiano-Reggiano cheese, shaved

Sformatini di Broccoletti con Mortadella

(Rapini Timbales with Mortadella Sausage)

SAUCE

3 carrots

3 ribs celery

4 onions

1 leek

8 cups water

2 bay leaves

4 to 5 parsley stems
(no leaves)

TIMBALES

1 bunch rapini

1 Tbsp. extra-virgin olive oil

1 Tbsp. + 2 tsp. chopped garlic

Pinch of chili flakes

2 eggs

2 Tbsp. shaved Parmigiano-
Reggiano cheese

1½ cups whipping cream

Pinch of nutmeg

2 Tbsp. sliced almonds

½ tsp. salt

4 oz. mortadella sausage,
julienned

THIS DISH is a variation on the usual *sformatino*, which is a vegetable dish made with eggs, baked in a mould and served with a sauce. The vegetables in this dish are delightfully sweet and contrast with the savoury timbale and mortadella. For variety, serve these timbales cold, surrounded by cold sauce and topped with crispy hot mortadella. Be careful not to oversalt the sauce. You can also serve this dish with mixed salad greens on the side.

SAUCE: Set aside 1 carrot, 1 rib celery and 1 onion. Roughly chop the remaining carrots, celery, onions and leek. Place in a stock-pot and add water, bay leaves and parsley. Bring to a boil on medium-high heat, then turn down the heat to low and simmer for 45 minutes. Strain through a fine-mesh sieve into a clean saucepan and discard the solids.

Finely dice the reserved carrot, celery and onion. Add them to the stock and cook on medium heat until for 20 to 30 minutes, until reduced to 10 per cent. Season with salt and pepper.

TIMBALES: Preheat the oven to 350°F. Grease 6 ramekins, each about 3¼ inches across and 2 inches deep. Line the bottom of each ramekin with parchment paper, then butter the paper.

Bring a large pot of salted water to a boil on high heat. Blanch rapini for 3 to 4 minutes, until tender, then drain.

Heat 2 tsp. of the oil in a frying pan on medium heat. Sauté rapini, garlic and chili flakes for 5 minutes, until any moisture evaporates. Transfer to a bowl and let cool. Purée in a food processor until fairly smooth.

In a bowl, whisk together puréed rapini, eggs, Parmigiano-Reggiano, cream, nutmeg, almonds, salt and a pinch of pepper. Fill the ramekins three quarters full with this custard mixture.

Set the ramekins in a large roasting pan and add enough hot water to reach halfway up the sides of the dishes. Bake in the oven for about 30 minutes, until custard is just set. Gently shake the ramekins, and if the custard jiggles slightly it is done. Remove from the oven and take out the ramekins from the roasting pan. Let cool.

While the timbales are cooking, heat the remaining oil in a frying pan on medium heat. Sauté mortadella until crispy. Use a slotted spoon to transfer mortadella to paper towels to drain.

TO SERVE: Reheat the sauce and reheat the ramekins in a 350°F oven for a few minutes (the water bath is not necessary). Run a knife around the edge of each ramekin. Place a plate over the top of each ramekin, then invert both the ramekin and the plate. Unmould the timbales, then remove the parchment paper. Garnish the timbales with mortadella and drizzle with sauce.

WINE: Savour a Mission Hill Pinot Grigio or one from Italy.

{ QUATTRO RESTAURANTS: *bradford ellis, robert parrott, jeremie trottier* }

Braised Rabbit and Saffron Cannelloni

Braised Rabbit and Saffron Cannelloni

YOU CAN MAKE the béchamel sauce and the rabbit filling a day ahead and refrigerate them overnight. You can also use fresh pasta sheets instead of making them yourself. Buy enough to make eighteen to twenty 4-inch squares. If you buy pasta, add the saffron to the rabbit filling. Assemble the entire dish in the morning, except for pouring the velouté sauce over top, then refrigerate until needed.

Taggiasche olives are small and dark green; they grow in the western Riviera. You can use niçoise or sun-dried Moroccan olives instead. *Serves 6*

BÉCHAMEL SAUCE: Heat milk in a saucepan on medium heat until it comes to a boil.

In another saucepan, melt butter on medium-low heat. Remove from the heat and stir in flour. Return to the heat and cook for 1 minute. Add hot milk all at once and whisk constantly until the mixture is smooth, thick and comes to a boil. Remove from the heat, then stir in salt and pepper.

Scrape the béchamel sauce into a bowl. Cover it with a piece of plastic wrap pressed right against the surface, to prevent a skin from forming. Refrigerate.

SAFFRON PASTA: Lightly dust a cookie sheet with semolina or all-purpose flour.

Place semolina in an electric mixer fitted with a dough hook.

In another bowl, whisk together oil, egg yolks and saffron. Pour the egg mixture slowly into the semolina and mix until the dough forms a solid ball. Transfer the dough to a lightly floured surface and knead briefly until it is firm but soft. Wrap the dough in plastic wrap and let set for at least 1 hour.

Roll the dough through a pasta machine, finishing with the thinnest setting, or use a rolling pin to roll it out to a thickness of ⅛ inch. Use a sharp knife to cut the pasta into 4-inch squares. Transfer them to the prepared cookie sheet, making sure not to overlap the squares. Cover the cookie sheet loosely with a tea towel until you are ready to cook the pasta.

Fill a large saucepan with salted water and bring to a rapid boil on high heat. Add the pasta squares and cook for 2 to 3 minutes, until al dente. Drain, then place in a clean container and cover with cold water until ready to fill the pasta. *continued overleaf >*

BÉCHAMEL SAUCE

1¾ cups milk

¼ cup butter

¼ cup all-purpose flour

¾ tsp. salt

¼ tsp. pepper

SAFFRON PASTA

1¼ cups semolina

2 tsp. olive oil

9 egg yolks

Pinch of saffron

FILLING

1 rabbit, about 2½ to 3 lbs.

2 Tbsp. vegetable oil

1 carrot, in small dice

1 onion, in small dice

2 ribs celery, in small dice

4 cups chicken stock, hot

1 bouquet garni
(1 bay leaf, 12 black peppercorns
and 2 sprigs fresh thyme
tied in cheesecloth)

4 oz. chanterelle mushrooms

1 tsp. toasted fennel seeds

¼ cup pitted and chopped
Taggiasche olives

¼ cup grated Parmigiano-
Reggiano cheese

VELOUTÉ SAUCE

2 Tbsp. butter

2 Tbsp. flour

½ cup peeled, deseeded
chopped tomatoes

1 tsp. chopped
fresh tarragon leaves

1 tsp. chopped
fresh oregano leaves

½ cup grated Parmigiano-
Reggiano, for garnish

FILLING: Preheat the oven to 325°F. Cut rabbit into quarters, then season with salt and black pepper. Heat 1 Tbsp. of the oil in a frying pan on medium-high heat. Sear rabbit for about 2 to 3 minutes per side, until browned. Transfer to a shallow ovenproof pan.

Add carrot, onion and celery to the frying pan on medium heat, then sauté for about 5 minutes, stirring often, until vegetables soften. Add vegetables to the rabbit, then cover with hot stock. Add bouquet garni, cover with a lid and braise in the oven for about 3 hours. (If the liquid boils rapidly, turn down the heat.) The rabbit is cooked when it is tender and nearly falling off the bones. Remove from the oven and let rabbit cool in the pan juices.

Transfer rabbit to a cutting board, but save the pan juices. Remove and discard all of the bones. (Work carefully because there are many tiny ones.) Shred rabbit meat and place in a bowl.

Strain pan juices through a fine-mesh sieve into a clean bowl.

Heat the remaining oil in a clean frying pan on medium-high heat. Sauté chanterelles for 5 minutes, until golden brown. Add to the rabbit meat. Mix in fennel seeds, olives, Parmigiano-Reggiano and enough béchamel sauce to bind the filling.

VELOUTÉ SAUCE: Melt butter in a saucepan on medium-low heat. Remove from the heat and stir in flour. Return to the heat and cook for 1 minute. Whisk in the reserved pan juices. Bring the sauce to a simmer and cook for about 20 minutes, until reduced to two thirds. Stir in tomatoes, tarragon and oregano.

FINISH CANNELLONI: Preheat the oven to 350°F. Drain and pat dry the pasta squares, if they have been held in water. Lay them out on a lightly floured surface. Place 2 Tbsp. of the rabbit filling along the bottom edge of each square, then roll up to make cannelloni.

Spoon a thin layer of velouté sauce into the bottom of a shallow baking dish that will hold all of the cannelloni in one layer. Place the cannelloni, seam side down, in a single layer. Cover with the remaining velouté sauce. Bake in the oven for about 15 minutes, until heated through.

TO SERVE: Place 2 or 3 cannelloni on individual plates. Garnish with Parmigiano-Reggiano.

WINE: Match with a big creamy white La Frenz Winery Chardonnay, or an elegant red Burrowing Owl Pinot Noir.

Porcini-crusted Halibut with Creamy Asparagus Sauce

Porcini-crusted Halibut

with Creamy Asparagus Sauce

PRAWN OIL

12 spot prawns, shells only

2 Tbsp. grapeseed oil

SAUCE

10 stalks green
asparagus, trimmed

½ cup whipping cream

1 shallot, sliced

1 clove garlic, mashed

1 Tbsp. butter

HALIBUT

2 oz. dried porcini
(cèpes) mushrooms

2 fillets halibut, each 5 oz.

1 Tbsp. vegetable oil

THIS RECIPE uses only the shells from prawns to make a flavour-ful oil that will keep in the refrigerator for up to 1 week. If you plan ahead, you can save uncooked prawn shells from another prawn dish by freezing them. If you buy fresh prawns for this recipe, you can turn the leftover prawn meat into an appetizer or another dish. Or you can replace the prawn oil in this recipe with your favourite herb oil.

For an elegant garnish, clean, destem and trim 12 chanterelle mushrooms. Sauté them in 2 tsp. vegetable oil on medium-high heat for 5 minutes. *Serves 2*

PRAWN OIL: Place prawn shells and grapeseed oil in a saucepan on medium heat. Cook for 5 to 8 minutes, until the shells turn red. Remove from the heat and let cool for 30 minutes. Strain through a fine-mesh sieve into a bowl and discard solids. Refrigerate until needed.

SAUCE: Peel asparagus stems and save the peelings. Place cream, shallot and garlic in a saucepan on medium heat. Bring to a sim-mer and cook for 5 to 6 minutes, until reduced to two thirds. Add asparagus peelings and cook for 2 minutes. Remove from the heat and let cool for 10 minutes. Purée in a blender. Strain through a fine-mesh sieve into a bowl and discard the solids. Season with salt and pepper. Keep warm.

Fill a bowl with ice water. Bring a pot of salted water to a boil, then blanch asparagus for about 4 minutes, until tender-crisp. Plunge asparagus immediately into the bowl of ice water to stop the cooking. When cool, drain and pat dry with paper towels.

HALIBUT: Place dried mushrooms in an electric coffee mill and grind to a powder. Season halibut with mushroom powder, salt and pepper.

Heat oil in a heavy frying pan on medium-high heat until nearly smoking. Gently place halibut in the pan, then turn down the heat to medium and sear for about 2 minutes per side, until golden. Continue cooking fish for 3 to 4 minutes, until it is just opaque. Transfer to a clean plate. Discard any excess oil but save the pan.

FINISH ASPARAGUS: Place the reserved frying pan on high heat and add butter. Sear asparagus on 1 side for about 2 minutes, until well browned.

TO SERVE: Spoon some asparagus sauce onto each plate. Place a piece of halibut on the sauce, then top with seared asparagus. Drizzle with prawn oil.

WINE: The asparagus, porcini and chanterelle mushrooms pair well with Hawthorne Mountain's See Ya Later Ranch Chardonnay.

Asian Pears in Phyllo
with Lavender Crème Chantilly

TARTS

¼ cup sugar, plus extra
for sprinkling on tart

1 lemon, juice of

½ cup water

2 Asian pears, peeled and
cored, in ½-inch slices

4 sheets frozen
phyllo pastry, thawed

½ cup unsalted
clarified butter

CRÈME CHANTILLY

½ cup whipping cream

2 sprigs fresh lavender
flowers, chopped

IF YOU DO NOT have tart pans, shape the phyllo into cups and place them on a cookie sheet before baking. *Serves 4*

TARTS: Place sugar, lemon juice and water in a saucepan on medium-high heat. Bring to a boil, then turn down the heat to medium-low. Add pears and poach for about 10 minutes, until they are tender but still hold their shape. Use a slotted spoon to transfer pears to a clean plate and let cool. Save the poaching syrup.

Preheat the oven to 350°F.

Lay 1 sheet of phyllo on a clean dry surface. (Keep the remaining sheets covered with plastic wrap or a lightly dampened cloth to prevent them drying out.) Brush a generous amount of clarified butter over the phyllo. Top with another sheet of phyllo and butter, then layer the 2 remaining phyllo sheets and butter. Cut phyllo into 4 circles about 4½ to 5 inches in diameter. Line four 3½ to 4-inch diameter tart pans with phyllo, pushing it gently into the corners.

Arrange pear slices in a spiral pattern on the phyllo, making sure to overlap each slice. Sprinkle lightly with sugar. Trim off any ragged bits of pastry (or leave the edges for a more rustic look), then bake in the oven for about 30 minutes, until phyllo is crisp and golden brown.

While the tarts are baking, place the reserved poaching syrup in a saucepan on medium heat. Cook for about 5 minutes, until the syrup thickens.

Remove the tarts from the oven and carefully brush the tops with thickened syrup to form a glaze. Let cool for 10 minutes.

CRÈME CHANTILLY: Place cream in the chilled bowl of an electric mixer and whip until stiff peaks form. Fold in lavender.

TO SERVE: Unmould tarts and place on individual plates. Garnish with a spoonful of crème chantilly.

WINE: Try drier Calliope Semillon with notes of beeswax, or the light Township 7 Pinot Blanc, both late harvest.

Pistachio-crusted Wild Arctic Muskox

with Porcini Cream Sauce

THE MUSKOX in this recipe is prepared rare; if you prefer your meat cooked medium or well-done, roast it for a longer time. Serve the muskox on spaetzle (page 125) or mashed potatoes, with cooked fresh fiddlehead greens on the side.

You can buy demi-glace in specialty food stores that sell stock. If you do not have demi-glace, use a concentrated stock: cook 3 cups chicken or veal stock on medium heat for 20 to 30 minutes, until reduced to 1 cup. *Serves 6*

SAUCE: Place dried mushrooms in a bowl and pour water over them. Let cool. Cover and refrigerate overnight. Drain the mushrooms and discard the soaking liquid.

Heat oil in a heavy saucepan on medium-high heat. Sauté mushrooms and shallots for 5 to 10 minutes, until soft and caramelized. Add brandy and vermouth, then deglaze the pan. Cook for about 10 minutes, until reduced to half. Stir in cream and demi-glace, then cook for about 15 to 20 minutes, until reduced to a creamy consistency. Remove from the heat and let cool for 10 minutes. Purée in a blender, then strain through a fine-mesh sieve into a clean bowl and discard the solids. Season with salt and pepper. Keep warm.

MUSKOX: Preheat the oven to 500°F. Season muskox with sea salt and freshly ground black pepper.

Heat oil in a frying pan on medium-high heat. Brown muskox for about 5 minutes per side. Transfer to a plate, then brush with butter. Roll muskox in pistachios, then place in a roasting pan and roast in the oven for about 5 minutes, until a meat thermometer inserted in the thickest part reads 125°F to 130°F. Remove from the oven and let rest for 5 to 10 minutes.

TO SERVE: Cut muskox into slices ¾-inch thick and place on individual plates. Drizzle with the mushroom sauce.

WINE: Serve with the opulent Black Hills Nota Bene, with its special aromas of cloves and nutmeg, made from Bordeaux-blend grapes grown near Oliver.

SAUCE

2 oz. dried porcini (cèpes) mushrooms or about 4 fresh

½ cup boiling water

1 Tbsp. vegetable oil

2 shallots, diced

2 Tbsp. brandy

½ cup vermouth or dry white wine

2 cups whipping cream

1 cup chicken or veal demi-glace

MUSKOX

2 lbs. muskox rib eye roast or beef rib eye steak, in one piece

2 Tbsp. vegetable oil

½ cup melted butter

½ cup ground pistachios

{ RIM ROCK CAFE & OYSTER BAR: *rolf gunter* }

Sticky Toffee Dessert

Sticky Toffee Dessert

THIS COMFORTING PUDDING lives up to its name! For an extra touch, garnish the dessert with a drizzle of chocolate sauce.

Serves 6 to 8

Preheat the oven to 350°F. Line an 8-inch springform pan with aluminum foil and butter it well.

    Place cream, 1 cup of the butter and 1¾ cups of the sugar in a saucepan on medium heat. Boil for 5 minutes, until the sauce begins to turn brown and thicken slightly. Pour half into the springform pan. Save the rest of the sauce.

    Place dried dates and baking soda in a bowl. Add boiling water, mix and let cool.

    Place the remaining butter, the remaining sugar and vanilla in an electric mixer. Beat on medium-high for about 5 minutes, until well creamed. Beat in egg, then stir in the date mixture.

    Combine flour and baking powder in a bowl. Fold into the egg mixture until evenly incorporated. Pour into the springform pan and bake in the oven for 30 minutes. Turn down the oven to 300°F and bake for 60 minutes, until golden brown and firm when touched lightly.

TO SERVE: Unmould the pudding, slice it and place slices on individual plates. Drizzle with the warmed reserved sauce.

WINE: Quails' Gate "FVF" Fortified Vintage Foch has incredible concentration and port richness to stand up to the sticky toffee.

1 cup whipping cream

1¼ cups unsalted butter

2¼ cups brown sugar

6 oz. dried dates, pitted

1 tsp. baking soda

1¼ cups boiling water

1 tsp. vanilla extract

1 egg

1½ cups all-purpose flour

1½ tsp. baking powder

Pan-seared Venison

on Barley-Potato Rosti with Cherry Jus

ROSTI

2 Tbsp. pearl barley, soaked in cold water to cover overnight

2 small to medium Yukon gold potatoes, peeled, one whole, one quartered

3 to 4 Tbsp. butter

1 Tbsp. olive oil

VENISON

1 cup fresh bread crumbs

1 cup wheat flakes

¼ cup chopped fresh parsley

2 Tbsp. + 1 tsp. wildflower honey

2 to 4 Tbsp. olive oil

4 portions venison loin, bone frenched if attached, each 4 to 5 oz.

1 Tbsp. butter

JUS

2 shallots, finely chopped

½ cup beef or veal stock

¼ cup Okanagan cherries, fresh or canned, pitted

A TENDER LOIN of venison, crusted with honey and wheat flakes, then served on a crisp barley-potato rosti and served with cherry jus, couldn't be a more local dish. Fry the rosti shortly after mixing in the raw shredded potato, so that they do not discolour. If necessary, you can reheat the rosti on a parchment-lined cookie sheet in a 350°F oven. Garnish each plate with seasonal vegetables. *Serves 4*

ROSTI: Drain barley and discard soaking water. Place barley and ½ cup water in a saucepan on medium-high heat. Bring to a boil, then turn down the heat to low and simmer for about 10 minutes, until barley is soft. Drain and place in a bowl.

Place the quartered potato with water to cover in a saucepan on medium heat. Bring to a boil and cook for about 15 minutes, until soft. Transfer to a bowl, add 2 to 3 Tbsp. of the butter and mash. Add to the barley and mix well.

Use a grater to finely shred the remaining raw potato. Add to the barley mixture, mixing gently so as not to break the potato shreds. Season with salt and pepper. Divide the mixture into 4 and form each portion into a patty about ¼-inch thick.

Place oil and the remaining butter in a frying pan on medium-high heat. Fry the rostis for about 5 minutes per side, until golden brown and crisp.

VENISON: Place bread crumbs, wheat flakes, parsley, 2 Tbsp. of the honey and 2 Tbsp. of the oil in a food processor. Pulse until the mixture is slightly moist and sticks together when pressed. If too crumbly, add 1 Tbsp. more of the olive oil. Transfer to a plate.

Preheat the oven to 350°F. Season the venison with salt and pepper.

Place the remaining oil and butter in an ovenproof pan on medium-high heat. Sear venison for 3 to 4 minutes per side, until well browned. Remove from the heat and brush with 1 tsp. of the honey. Roll venison in the bread crumb mixture, then return to the pan and roast in the oven for about 10 minutes, until done. (Venison is most tender when done rare or medium-rare, 135° to 140°F on a meat thermometer. A fingertip lightly pressed on top should meet with some resistance but not be firm.) Remove from the oven and set aside in a warm place. Save the pan.

JUS: Place the reserved pan on medium heat and sauté shallots for about 5 minutes, until translucent. Add stock and deglaze the pan. Cook for 5 minutes to reduce sauce a little. Stir in cherries, then season with salt and pepper.

TO SERVE: Carve venison into 8 to 12 slices, or if using loin chops, serve one per person. Place a rosti on each plate and top with 2 to 3 slices of venison. Drizzle with cherry jus.

WINE: Mission Hill Cabernet Sauvignon Family Estate Reserve has lovely cherry fruit to match this dish.

Lemon Rice

CURRY LEAVES are sold in Indian specialty markets. Turmeric gives the rice its beautiful yellow colour. *Serves 4*

Heat oil in a nonstick frying pan on medium heat. Sauté mustard seeds and chili pepper for 1 minute, until mustard seeds start to pop. Stir in steamed rice and curry leaves, then sauté for 1 minute. Add turmeric, season with salt and mix well. Stir in lemon juice and green onions, then sauté for 1 minute.

TO SERVE: Transfer to a serving bowl.

WINE: Pair with the Sauvignon Blanc and Chardonnay blend from Thornhaven Estates Vineyard and Winery in Summerland.

2 tsp. vegetable oil

½ tsp. mustard seeds

1 dried red chili pepper

3 cups steamed basmati rice

2 Indian curry leaves

¼ tsp. turmeric

1 tsp. lemon juice

10 green onions, chopped

Carrot-Ginger-Mint Chutney

CHANNA DAL are yellow split peas, sold in Indian specialty markets. Be sure to look through them and remove any small stones before you cook them.

This chutney will keep refrigerated for up to 10 days. You can also serve it as a side dish with crab cakes or sesame-crusted scallops. *Serves 8*

Heat oil in a frying pan on medium heat and sauté mustard seeds for 2 minutes, until they begin to pop. Stir in channa dal and cook for about 3 minutes, until the dal browns. Stir in carrots, ginger, water, sugar and garam masala. Season with salt, then cook partially covered with a lid for 6 to 10 minutes, until carrots and dal are soft.

Remove from the heat, then stir in coriander seeds (and mint if using dried). Let cool. (Add mint now if using fresh.) Transfer to a blender, add buttermilk and process to a fine paste. Scrape into a small bowl, cover with plastic wrap and refrigerate until needed.

TO SERVE: Spoon a little on the side of each plate or place in a small serving bowl.

WINE: Served with crab cakes or scallops, the Mission Hill Family Estate Pinot Gris Reserve with a touch of oak balances the chutney.

½ cup canola oil

¼ cup mustard seeds

½ cup channa dal

3 carrots, chopped

1 tsp. minced fresh ginger

1 cup water

1 tsp. sugar

¼ tsp. garam masala

¼ tsp. coriander seeds

¼ cup chopped fresh mint
or 2 tsp. dried mint

1 cup buttermilk

Saffron Cream Yogurt with Pistachio Nuts

4 cups thick,
extra cream yogurt

½ cup berry (extra-fine) sugar

¼ tsp. ground cardamom

2 Tbsp. whipping cream

Pinch of saffron powder

2 Tbsp. crushed pistachio
nuts, for garnish

THIS IS A LIGHT and refreshing dessert. If you cannot find thick yogurt, make your own. Place thin yogurt in a clean cloth, gather the corners and tie closed with kitchen string, leaving enough string to tie the pouch to a rack in the refrigerator. Place a bowl underneath the pouch to catch the excess liquid and let the yogurt drain for several hours or overnight. Discard liquid.

Instead of pistachio, you can garnish this dish with slices of fresh mango, frozen grapes or pomegranate seeds. *Serves 6 to 8*

Whisk together yogurt and sugar in a bowl until well combined. Add cardamom and mix well.

Place cream and saffron in a bowl and warm in a microwave oven on medium for 1 minute. Fold into the drained yogurt, then cover and refrigerate until well chilled.

TO SERVE: Spoon into individual serving bowls and dust with pistachios.

WINE: Jackson-Triggs Proprietors' Grand Reserve Sparkling Riesling Icewine provides sweetness with refreshing bubbles.

{ RUBINA TANDOORI: *krishna jamal* }

Saffron Cream Yogurt with Pistachio Nuts

{ SEASONS IN THE PARK: *lynda larouche* }

Organic Carrot Soup

Organic Carrot Soup

THIS VELVETY SOUP can be served hot or chilled. Use the full ⅓ cup of oil, which gives the soup its lovely velvety texture. You can garnish the soup with a dollop of whipped cream and a sprinkle of finely chopped chives. *Serves 6*

⅓ cup organic olive oil

1 onion, chopped

2 lbs. organic carrots, chopped

4 cups unchlorinated natural spring water

Heat oil in a saucepan on medium-high heat. Sauté onion and carrots for 5 to 7 minutes, until the aroma fills the air. Add water and bring to a boil, then turn down the heat to low and simmer, with the lid partially on, for about 45 minutes, until vegetables are soft. Let cool slightly. Purée in batches, while holding a folded towel on top of the lid of the blender. Season with salt and pepper.

Refrigerate the soup for serving later or gently reheat and serve. The soup will keep in the refrigerator for up to 4 days.

TO SERVE: Pour reheated soup into a tureen or soup bowls.

WINE: Serve this soup on its own or with Brights "74" or Pale Dry Select sherry.

West Coast Fish Cakes with Gold Pineapple Relish

RELISH

2 cups finely diced pineapple

¼ red onion, finely diced

2 tsp. chopped fresh cilantro

2 Tbsp. chopped fresh basil

2 Tbsp. freshly
squeezed orange juice

½ jalapeño pepper, minced

FISH CAKES

2 Tbsp. vegetable oil

½ medium to large
onion, minced

1 cup cooked fresh
shrimp meat, about 4½ oz.

1 cup salmon, in ½-inch
cubes, about 4½ oz.

1 cup cod, in ½-inch
cubes, about 4½ oz.

4 egg whites

1 tsp. chopped parsley

4 small red potatoes,
cooked in skins, then peeled,
cooled and grated

1 Tbsp. chopped roasted garlic

1 cup fresh bread crumbs

HAWAII'S GOLD PINEAPPLES are very sweet and work particularly well in this recipe. For variety, use passion fruit juice instead of the orange juice in the pineapple relish. The relish will keep for up to 5 days in the refrigerator.

Serve with a mixed green salad lightly dressed with vinaigrette. *Serves 6*

RELISH: Combine pineapple, onion, cilantro, basil, orange juice and jalapeño pepper in a bowl. Mix well, then season with kosher salt and black pepper. Refrigerate for 2 hours to allow the flavours to blend.

FISH CAKES: Heat 1 Tbsp. of the oil in a saucepan on medium heat and sauté onion for about 5 minutes, until transparent. Let cool.

Combine onion, shrimp, salmon, cod, egg whites, parsley, potatoes and garlic. Season with salt and pepper. Mix well, then shape into 18 patties, each ½-inch thick. Coat patties evenly with bread crumbs.

Heat the remaining oil in a frying pan on medium heat. Gently fry fish cakes, in batches, for about 4 minutes per side, until golden and cooked through. (Place cooked fish cakes on a cookie sheet and keep them warm in a 200°F oven while you fry the rest.) Drain on paper towels.

TO SERVE: Place 3 fish cakes and a couple of spoonfuls of relish on each serving plate.

WINE: Zanatta Winery on Vancouver Island has the green apple Glenora Fantasia Brut from Cayuga grapes, or raspberry and kiwi Allegria Brut Rosé from Pinot Noir and Auxerrois.

{ SOOKE HARBOUR HOUSE: *edward tuson* }

Wild Chanterelle Mushroom, Walnut and Summer Savory Soup with Nasturtium Flower Cream

Wild Chanterelle Mushroom, Walnut and Summer Savory Soup
with Nasturtium Flower Cream

FOR A LOVELY CONTRAST to the soup, use only yellow nasturtium flowers in the cream. Use other edible flowers, if nasturtiums are not available, to garnish the soup. *Serves 6*

CREAM: Place flowers and cream in an electric mixer. Whip until stiff peaks form. Cover and refrigerate the cream for up to 1 hour.

SOUP: Melt butter in a large stainless steel saucepan on medium heat. Add onions, carrots, celery, mushrooms, walnuts, fennel seeds, coriander seeds and cumin seeds. Sauté for 10 to 15 minutes, until onion is translucent and carrots begin to soften. Add garlic and ginger, the sauté for 5 minutes, stirring constantly to prevent burning.

Add wine, then turn up the heat to high. Cook for about 5 minutes, until ¼ cup of the liquid remains. Stir in bay leaves, savory, stock and cream, then bring to a boil. Turn down the heat to low and simmer for 25 minutes, until vegetables are soft. Remove from the heat and let cool for 30 minutes.

Purée in small batches in a blender. Return to the saucepan and reheat on low heat.

TO SERVE: Ladle hot soup into individual bowls. Top each serving with about 2 Tbsp. of the cream.

WINE: A lovely match with Andrés almond cream or golden cream sherry.

CREAM

½ cup chopped organic nasturtium flowers, stems removed

½ cup whipping cream

SOUP

¼ cup unsalted butter

1 cup diced onions

½ cup diced carrots

½ cup diced celery

2 cups chopped chanterelle mushrooms

½ cup walnut meat

½ tsp. fennel seeds

¼ tsp. coriander seeds

¼ tsp. cumin seeds

2 Tbsp. chopped garlic

2 Tbsp. minced fresh ginger

½ cup dry white wine

2 bay leaves, fresh or dry

2 Tbsp. fresh summer savory leaves

5 cups chicken stock

1 cup whipping cream

Oven-dried Apple and Pear Rings

1 unpeeled organic apple,
cored, in ⅛-inch thick rings

1 unpeeled organic
Anjou pear, cored,
in ⅛-inch thick rings

½ cup icing sugar

THESE RINGS of dried fruit make a lovely garnish for a salad or a dessert. Leaving the skin on the fruit helps to prevent shrinkage. The dried fruit will keep in an airtight container in a cool, dry place for up to 6 months.

Preheat the oven to 250°F. Place a stainless steel cooling rack on a cookie sheet and cover the rack with a sheet of parchment paper.

Place fruit rings in a single layer on the parchment paper and sprinkle liberally with icing sugar. Bake for about 75 minutes, until the fruit is light golden brown, dry and crisp. Remove from the oven and let cool.

Lavender, Maple and Carrot Ice Milk

CRISP COOKIES are a perennial favourite with ice cream; try a simple butter cookie with the complex flavours of this dessert. Garnish each serving with ½ tsp. maple syrup and a sprig of lavender florets. *Serves 8*

CARROT PURÉE: Combine all the ingredients in a stainless steel saucepan on high heat. Bring to a boil, then turn down the heat to medium-low and simmer for 35 to 40 minutes, until carrots are soft. Remove from the heat and let cool for 20 minutes. Purée in a blender, then strain through a fine-mesh sieve and discard the solids.

ICE MILK: Place carrot purée and milk in a saucepan, then whisk until smooth. Stir in lavender and bring to a boil on medium heat. Remove from the heat and keep warm.

Whisk together egg yolks, sugar, brown sugar and maple syrup in a stainless steel bowl. Place the bowl over a saucepan of simmering but not boiling water on low heat. Whisk for 15 to 20 minutes, until the mixture is thick and just hot. Remove from the heat.

Fill a large bowl with ice water. Slowly whisk a little of the carrot mixture into the egg mixture. Stir in the remaining carrot mixture. Place the bowl over the saucepan of simmering but not boiling water on low heat. Stir constantly for about 5 minutes, until the mixture thickens and coats the back of a spoon.

Remove from the heat and place the bowl over the bowl of ice water. Keep stirring until the mixture is cool, then stir in brandy. Strain through a fine-mesh sieve into a clean bowl and discard the solids. Refrigerate for 3 to 4 hours, until very cold. Process in an ice-cream maker according to the manufacturer's instructions.

TO SERVE: Place 3 small scoops in each dessert dish.

WINE: The maple with lavender and rosemary suits Lang Vineyard's unusual Canadian Maple Brut sparkling wine.

CARROT PURÉE

1 lb. carrots (preferably organic), peeled, in 1-inch pieces

1 Tbsp. fresh rosemary or 2 tsp. dried rosemary

1 cup apple juice

2 Tbsp. golden brown sugar

ICE MILK

2 cups 2% milk

1½ tsp. lavender florets

8 egg yolks

¼ cup sugar

¼ cup golden brown sugar

½ cup maple syrup

2 Tbsp. brandy

Parsnip and Roasted Garlic Cheesecakes
with Candied Walnuts

CANDIED WALNUTS

1 egg white (use the yolk
for cheesecake)

2 Tbsp. brown sugar

¾ cup walnut meat (whole or
halves, preferably organic)

CHEESECAKES

1 ¼ cups granola
(preferably not too sweet)

2 Tbsp. butter, softened, plus
more to grease the ramekins

½ cup + 2 Tbsp. parsnip purée

4 oz. cream cheese

2 Tbsp. sour cream

2 cloves roasted garlic

2 eggs

1 egg yolk

1 Tbsp. finely chopped
fresh thyme

¼ tsp. nutmeg

SALAD

2 cups salad greens

2 Tbsp. olive oil

4 Tbsp. beet chips (optional)

THE WALNUTS can be candied ahead of time and stored in an airtight container for up to 2 weeks. Beet chips are sold in health food stores.

To make parsnip purée, place 2 peeled parsnips with enough cold water to cover them in a saucepan on high heat and boil for about 15 minutes, until tender, then drain and purée them in a food processor. *Serves 4*

CANDIED WALNUTS: Preheat the oven to 350°F.

Whisk egg white in a large bowl until it loses its opaqueness and turns white. Stir in sugar, then add walnuts and toss well. Pour off any excess egg white that may be clinging to the walnuts, then spread them out on a cookie sheet. Bake in the oven for 15 to 20 minutes, stirring every 5 minutes, until dry.

CHEESECAKES: Preheat the oven to 300°F. Lightly butter four ½-cup ramekins or four 3½-inch ring moulds.

Grind granola and butter in a food processor until well mixed. Divide the mixture evenly among the ramekins, then press down firmly to make a crust.

Combine parsnip purée, cream cheese, sour cream, garlic, eggs, egg yolk, thyme and nutmeg in a food processor. Season with salt and black pepper, then mix until smooth. Be sure to scrape down the sides of the bowl. Pour into the ramekins over the bases, then bake in the oven for about 20 minutes, until the centres are firm to the touch. Remove from the oven and let cool slightly. Run a knife around the edge of the cheesecakes, then unmould them.

SALAD: Just before serving, place salad greens in a serving bowl. Add olive oil and toss well. Garnish with candied walnuts and beet chips (optional).

TO SERVE: Place a warm cheesecake on each plate. Top with a mound of salad.

WINE: Sip Gehringer Brothers Schonburger-Gewurztraminer Classic, with its hint of spicy sweetness, as an aperitif, then follow it with this hors d'oeuvre.

Parsnip and Roasted Garlic Cheesecakes with Candied Walnuts

Red and Yellow Tomato Salad with Seared Asparagus and Saltspring Island Goat Cheese

Red and Yellow Tomato Salad

with Seared Asparagus and Saltspring Island Goat Cheese

LATE SUMMER is the perfect time to make this savoury salad. Watch for heirloom varieties of tomatoes—in a range of colours—at farmers' markets. *Serves 4*

Cut tomatoes into slices ¼-inch thick and arrange in a single layer on a large platter. Drizzle with extra-virgin olive oil and vinegar, season with fleur de sel and freshly ground black pepper, then sprinkle with shallots. Let marinate for several minutes.

Fill a saucepan with salted water and bring to a boil on high heat. Add asparagus and blanch for 60 seconds, until bright green. Transfer to paper towels and pat dry.

Heat oil in a frying pan on high heat. Sear asparagus, turning often, for 2 minutes, until just tender. Transfer to a plate and let cool.

TO SERVE: Arrange tomatoes and asparagus on each plate. Cut goat cheese into 1-inch wedges and place on top. Drizzle cheese and the plate with the marinade from the tomatoes. Garnish with basil.

WINE: Sumac Ridge is the pioneer of Sauvignon Blanc in the Okanagan, so try its herbal gooseberry White Label.

3 vine-ripened red tomatoes, blanched, peeled

3 vine-ripened yellow tomatoes, blanched, peeled

½ cup extra-virgin olive oil

¼ cup balsamic vinegar

Fleur de sel

2 shallots, very finely chopped

12 stalks asparagus, trimmed

1 Tbsp. olive oil

1 Saltspring Island goat cheese, about 4 to 4½ oz.

Fresh basil leaves for garnish

Organic Lavender Shortbread
with Summer Berries and Black Pepper Whipped Cream

½ cup unsalted butter,
room temperature

¼ cup sugar

1 tsp. organic fresh
lavender flowers

1 tsp. lemon zest

1 cup all-purpose flour

3 Tbsp. rice flour

2 cups blackberries

2 cups blueberries

2 cups strawberries,
hulled and quartered

2 Tbsp. Grand Marnier

1¼ cups whipping cream,
whipped to soft peaks

Icing sugar for dusting

4 fresh mint leaves
for garnish

IF YOU CANNOT FIND organic lavender flowers, order them from www.tuscanfarmgardens.com. *Serves 4*

Preheat the oven to 350°F. Line a cookie sheet with parchment paper.

Cream butter well, then beat in sugar until the mixture is light in colour. Stir in lavender and lemon zest.

Sift all-purpose and rice flours together into a bowl. Gradually add to the butter mixture, mixing well until thoroughly combined. Gather the dough and form it into a ball.

Generously flour a work surface and roll out dough to a thickness of ⅛ inch. Use a round 3-inch diameter cookie cutter to cut out 12 rounds. Place them on the prepared cookie sheet and bake in the oven for 10 to 12 minutes, until barely coloured. Let cool slightly, then transfer to a wire rack to cool completely.

Combine blackberries (save 4 for garnish), blueberries and strawberries in a bowl. Sprinkle with Grand Marnier.

TO SERVE: Place a shortbread in the middle of each plate, then top with some berries and a spoonful of whipped cream. Top with a second shortbread, pressing down gently. Add another layer of berries and another spoonful of whipped cream. Finish with a third shortbread, then sift a dusting of icing sugar over it. Finish with a final dollop of whipped cream and sprinkle with freshly cracked black pepper. Garnish with a reserved blackberry and a mint leaf.

WINE: The berries work well with either the blueberry or strawberry dessert wine from Westham Island Estate Winery.

Shrimp Cakes
with Seasonal Baby Mesclun Salad and Two Dressings

THIS DISH pairs a wasabi vinaigrette with a light soy and mirin sauce over seasonal baby greens. For the white fish in this recipe, use halibut, snapper or cod. *Serves 4*

SHRIMP CAKES: Place dashi, carrot, onion and mushrooms in a saucepan on medium heat. Cook for about 10 minutes, until vegetables soften. Stir gently then remove from the heat and let cool.

Place cooled vegetables, shrimp, fish, sea salt, soy sauce and sugar in a food processor. Pulse until well blended. Add half of the beaten egg and mix until it is a sticky paste. Transfer to a bowl, cover with plastic wrap and refrigerate for 30 to 60 minutes. Discard the other half of the beaten egg.

Divide the shrimp mixture into 4 portions and form each one into a patty about ½- to ¾-inch thick. Heat oil in a frying pan on medium-low heat and fry the patties for 4 to 5 minutes per side, until golden brown. Drain on paper towels.

VINAIGRETTE: Whisk together wasabi and mayonnaise in a bowl until well blended. Slowly whisk in mirin and vinegar. Add white pepper to taste.

SAUCE: Combine dashi, mirin, soy sauce and sugar in a saucepan on medium heat. Mix well. Add cornstarch mixture and bring to a boil, whisking constantly until it thickens. Remove from the heat and keep warm.

SALAD: Place a mound of mesclun in the middle of each plate and sprinkle with shiso.

TO SERVE: Cut warm shrimp cakes into ½-inch strips and arrange on the salad. Drizzle wasabi vinaigrette and soy-mirin sauce over and around the shrimp cakes and salad. Garnish with a pinch of bonito flakes and some daikon sprouts.

WINE: Lovely with Hawthorne Mountain HMV Brut.

SHRIMP CAKES
2 Tbsp. dashi (page 180)

2 Tbsp. finely diced carrot

½ small onion, finely chopped

2 large fresh shiitake mushrooms, destemmed and finely diced

6 oz. large raw shrimp, peeled, deveined, coarsely chopped

4 oz. white-fleshed fish, deboned, coarsely chopped

½ tsp. sea salt

1 tsp. light soy sauce

2 tsp. sugar

1 large egg, well beaten

2 Tbsp. vegetable oil

VINAIGRETTE
1 Tbsp. wasabi paste

1 Tbsp. mayonnaise

1 Tbsp. mirin (page 13)

1 Tbsp. rice vinegar

SAUCE
¼ cup dashi (page 180)

2 Tbsp. + 2 tsp. mirin

2 Tbsp. + 2 tsp. dark soy sauce

1 tsp. sugar

1 tsp. cornstarch mixed with 1 Tbsp. water

SALAD
2 cups fresh baby mesclun or seasonal baby lettuce

4 shiso leaves, finely julienned

Dried bonito flakes for garnish

Daikon sprouts, bottoms trimmed off, for garnish

Kunsei Gindara

(Smoked Sablefish in Parchment)

FILLING

FILLING

¼ cup dashi

1 Tbsp. light soy sauce

1 Tbsp. mirin (page 13)

4 large shiitake mushrooms,
destemmed and cut
in ⅛-inch slices

4 thick stalks asparagus,
trimmed, peeled,
tips removed

1 underripe mango,
peeled, in pieces
½ × ½ × 3½ inches

FISH

1 lb. smoked sablefish fillets,
1-inch thick, in 4 pieces

2 Tbsp. vegetable oil

BE SURE to use smoked fish in this recipe. If you cannot find smoked sablefish, look for it labelled as lightly smoked Alaska black cod. Dashi is a stock made from dried bonito tuna flakes, sold in Japanese specialty stores. If you cannot find it, use chicken or fish stock. *Serves 4*

FILLING: Combine dashi, soy sauce and mirin in a saucepan on medium heat. Add mushrooms and cook gently for 2 to 3 minutes, until slightly soft. Strain through a fine-mesh sieve into a clean saucepan and save the liquid. Place mushrooms in a bowl and let cool.

Cut asparagus stalks in 1-inch lengths and place in the reserved cooking liquid. Cook on medium heat for about 2 minutes, until soft but still firm. Drain and let cool.

FISH: Preheat the oven to 450°F. Cut 4 sheets of parchment paper or aluminum foil, each 12 inches square. Lightly brush the middle of the paper or foil with oil.

Double-fillet the fish by making two horizontal cuts, so that each piece opens up like a two-fold brochure into one long piece about ⅓ the thickness of the original piece. To do this, place a fillet on a cutting board, with the grain of the fish parallel to the top edge of the board. Insert the blade of a sharp knife at one edge of the fillet, about ⅓ down from its surface. Make a horizontal (butterfly) cut through the fillet, stopping about ⅓ inch before the opposite edge. (Be very careful not to cut all the way through the fillet.) At the end of this first cut, cut down ⅓ inch, then slice horizontally, parallel to the first cut, but going in the opposite direction, and stop without cutting all the way through the fillet. Repeat with the remaining fillets.

Carefully open up the butterflied layers of each fillet. Arrange mushrooms, asparagus and mango in the centre of each. Fold one flap over the filling, then fold the other flap over the first one. Place each fillet, seam side down, on a piece of parchment paper.

Bring together the top and bottom ends of the parchment paper, then fold over together to make a single tight fold, as if you were gift-wrapping a parcel. Fold down the sides of the parchment and tuck them underneath. Place the parcels on a cookie sheet and bake in the middle of the oven for 10 minutes.

TO SERVE: Place each parcel on a warmed plate. Just before serving, carefully unfold the parcel.

WINE: Pair with Hillside Estate Gewurztraminer (with a touch of Scheurebe), or its Pinot Gris Reserve, which uses oak (some Hungarian) in a Baden style.

Garam Masala-sautéed Portobello Mushrooms
in Porcini Cream Curry

PORCINI CREAM CURRY

2 heaping Tbsp. dried porcini
(cèpes) mushrooms

3 Tbsp. canola or olive oil

1 onion, finely chopped

2 Tbsp. + 2 tsp. all-purpose flour

½ cup whipping cream

1 heaping tsp. dried
green fenugreek leaves

½ tsp. salt

¼ tsp. cayenne pepper

MUSHROOMS

6 large portobello
mushrooms, destemmed

4 Tbsp. canola or olive oil

¼ tsp. asafoetida powder

1 Tbsp. mango powder

1 Tbsp. garam masala

¼ tsp. cayenne pepper

¾ tsp. salt

VISIT YOUR local Indian specialty store before making this dish. You will need *hing* (asafoetida), *amchur* (mango powder) and *kasuri methi* (dried green fenugreek). Prepare the portobello mushrooms while the curry is cooking. Be careful not to overcook the mushrooms when you sauté them, as they will continue to cook when you pour the hot curry over them. *Serves 6 as an appetizer*

PORCINI CREAM CURRY: Place mushrooms and 1 cup of very hot water in a bowl and let sit for 30 minutes.

Heat oil in a frying pan on medium heat and sauté onion for 10 minutes, until brown. Remove from the heat and stir in flour. Return to the heat and cook for 2 minutes, until flour is light brown. Stir in mushrooms and their soaking water, 1½ cups water, cream, fenugreek, salt and cayenne. Bring to a low boil and cook for about 20 minutes. Keep warm on lowest heat.

MUSHROOMS: Cut each mushroom into 5 or 6 slices. Heat oil in a frying pan on medium heat. Sprinkle asafoetida into the pan and let it sizzle for 30 seconds. Immediately add mango powder, garam masala, cayenne and salt, then cook, while stirring, for 1 to 2 minutes. The spices will foam lightly. Add mushrooms and sauté, stirring constantly, for 3 minutes, until fork-tender.

TO SERVE: Divide the mushrooms among plates, then top each serving with a sixth of the hot curry sauce.

WINE: The spiciness of the garam masala goes well with the white peppery, smoky aromas of Mission Hill's well-balanced Syrah, or La Frenz Syrah made from either Sierra Oaks Vineyard Fairplay fruit or Estate Fiddletown.

Prawns in Coconut Milk

Y OU WILL NEED about two pounds of prawns for this dish. Be very careful not to overcook them. *Serves 6*

Rub prawns with salt, then place in a bowl, cover and refrigerate.

Melt ghee in a frying pan on medium heat and sauté onions for about 15 minutes, until brown and soft. Stir in cumin seeds and cook for 2 to 3 minutes, until they turn a darker colour. Stir in tomatoes, coconut milk, vinegar and chilies, then cook for about 10 minutes, until tomatoes are cooked through. Add green onions and prawns, then cook for about 5 minutes, stirring constantly, until prawns are opaque, slightly pink and firm to the touch. Season to taste with salt.

TO SERVE: Serve in small individual bowls or on a colourful appetizer platter.

WINE: Blue Mountain Rose Brut Sparkling has both wonderful colour and flavour, or try the crisp refreshing Quails' Gate Chenin Blanc.

30 tiger prawns, shelled and deveined

1 tsp. salt

2 Tbsp. ghee (page 111)

2 large onions, chopped

½ tsp. cumin seeds

3 large tomatoes, peeled, deseeded and finely chopped

2 Tbsp. coconut milk

2 Tbsp. red wine vinegar

2 tsp. green chilies, finely chopped

1 bunch green onions, chopped

{ **VIJ'S**: *vikram vij* }

Marinated Lamb Popsicles with Fenugreek Cream Curry

Marinated Lamb Popsicles
with Fenugreek Cream Curry

THIS DELICIOUS CURRY SAUCE may be doubled and used to enhance other meat, poultry or fish dishes. *Serves 6*

LAMB: Combine wine, mustard and salt in a large bowl or in a large resealable plastic freezer bag. Add lamb and coat well with the marinade. Cover the bowl (or seal the bag and place it in a bowl) and marinate in the refrigerator for 2 to 3 hours.

CURRY SAUCE: Combine cream, salt, cayenne, paprika, fenugreek and lemon juice in a bowl.

Heat oil in a heavy saucepan on medium heat and sauté garlic for about 2 minutes, until golden. Stir in turmeric and cook for 1 minute. Stir in the cream mixture and cook on low to medium heat for a few minutes, until well blended and hot.

FINISH LAMB: Preheat a barbecue or a broiler to high heat. Place lamb on the grill and cook for 3 to 5 minutes per side, until medium, or medium-rare.

TO SERVE: Arrange lamb popsicles on a serving platter. Either pour curry over them or serve it in small bowls on the side.

WINE: Try the complementary punch of CedarCreek's jammy Merlot, or its Platinum Reserve Meritage with ripe red berries and a touch of anise.

LAMB
¼ cup dry white wine

¼ cup grainy Dijon mustard

¾ tsp. salt

2 to 3 lamb racks, each 2 lbs., cut into chops, ends of bones trimmed clean of meat

CURRY SAUCE
2 cups whipping cream

¼ tsp. salt

¼ tsp. cayenne pepper

⅛ tsp. paprika

1½ tsp. dried green fenugreek (page 182)

2 Tbsp. fresh lemon juice

1 to 2 Tbsp. canola oil

1 Tbsp. crushed garlic

½ tsp. turmeric

Caramella di Spinachi
(Candy-wrapped Spinach and Mascarpone Pasta)

FILLING

2 lbs. spinach,
large stems removed

½ tsp. coarse salt

1 cup mascarpone cheese

½ cup freshly grated
Parmigiano-Reggiano

3 large egg yolks

Pinch of freshly
grated nutmeg

PASTA

1 lb. fresh pasta dough
(page 151), omit the saffron,
or 6 sheets fresh lasagne

1 large egg, beaten

Pinch of coarse salt

GARNISH

1 cup unsalted butter
or 1 cup light tomato sauce

1 cup freshly grated
Parmigiano-Reggiano cheese

10 large basil leaves
for garnish

THE BUTTER SAUCE in this recipe is optional. If you prefer, replace it with a light tomato sauce. If you do not have mascarpone cheese, substitute ½ cup ricotta blended with 1 cup whipping cream.

The filled pasta can be made a few hours ahead and stored in the refrigerator, covered, or it will keep in the freezer for up to 1 week. Allow frozen pasta to thaw at room temperature, covered with plastic wrap, turning each piece 1 or 2 times before cooking. *Serves 6*

FILLING: Soak spinach in a bowl of cold water for 30 minutes. Drain.

Bring a large pot of cold water to boil on high heat. Add salt and spinach, then cook for a few minutes, until wilted. Drain spinach in a colander and cool under cold running water.

Squeeze cooled spinach dry, then chop finely and place in a nonreactive bowl. Add mascarpone, Parmigiano-Reggiano and egg yolks, then mix well with a wooden spoon. Season with nutmeg, salt and pepper, then mix well. Cover with plastic wrap and refrigerate for 3 to 4 hours.

PASTA: Lightly flour a work surface. Roll out pasta dough to a thickness of ⅛ inch. Sprinkle dough with additional flour, then roll out to a thickness of 1⁄16 inch. Cut into rectangles, each about 4½ × 5½ inches. Brush each rectangle with beaten egg.

Place 1 heaping Tbsp. of the filling in the middle of each rectangle. Fold the left third of the pasta over the filling, then fold the right third of the pasta over the left. Grasp the top and bottom ends of the pasta, then twist them in opposite directions to make a shape resembling a wrapped candy. Arrange the filled pasta on a lightly floured nonstick surface or a cotton towel, making sure they do not touch. Let rest for 30 to 60 minutes, turning once or twice.

Bring a large pot of cold water to a boil on medium-high heat. Stir in coarse salt, then add the filled pasta, a few at a time, and cook for 2 to 4 minutes, until al dente. (Check that the pasta is cooked by cutting into one cooked piece; if the pasta is tender and the filling is hot, it is done.)

TO SERVE: While pasta is cooking, melt butter in a saucepan on low heat and pour onto a warm serving platter. Use a slotted spoon to transfer the first batch of cooked pasta to the serving platter. Sprinkle with Parmigiano-Reggiano. Repeat this layering until all of the pasta is cooked. Garnish with basil leaves.

WINE: Hillside Estate Merlot Reserve is rich and intense enough for the spinach, mascarpone and Parmigiano-Reggiano.

{ VILLA DEL LUPO: *julio gonzalez-perini* }

Angelica's Roasted Chicken with Mustard and Cinzano Sauce

Angelica's Roasted Chicken
with Mustard and Cinzano Sauce

IF YOU DON'T WANT to debone a chicken, or if you wish to serve four people, substitute four boneless chicken half breasts or a larger whole chicken for the one here. Just remember to adjust the cooking times and to make one and a half times more sauce. Serve this chicken with steamed vegetables and roasted potatoes. *Serves 2*

CHICKEN: Place cognac, thyme and bay leaves in a large bowl. Add chicken and marinate for 1 hour. Cover and refrigerate. Take out of the refrigerator and remove chicken from the marinade 30 minutes before roasting.

Preheat the oven to 350°F. Grease a roasting pan.

Insert half of the garlic and rosemary in the thigh cavity of each half of the deboned chicken, lay 1 leg bone in each half, then wrap the breast around the entire thigh. Pressing forward, fold the skin over the meat as tightly as possible to give the chicken a pear shape. Pull up the leg bone. If doing breasts or a whole chicken, free up the skin from the flesh using your fingers, then insert herbs between the skin and breast meat.

Tie each chicken half with kitchen string. Wrap the end of each leg bone with aluminum foil to prevent it from burning. Place chicken halves, leg bone up, in the roasting pan. Brush with melted butter, then season with salt and pepper. Roast for 30 to 40 minutes, until cooked through. Remove from the oven and let sit for 5 minutes.

SAUCE: Heat stock and vermouth in a saucepan on medium-high heat. Cook for about 10 minutes, until reduced to three quarters. Whisk in mustard and butter.

TO SERVE: Place a chicken half on each warmed plate and drizzle sauce over it.

WINE: Burrowing Owl's special Cabernet Franc suits this chicken, as does its Cabernet Sauvignon.

CHICKEN
½ cup cognac

2 sprigs fresh thyme

2 bay leaves

1 small free-range chicken, about 2½ lbs., deboned and cut in half (save 2 of the leg bones)

2 cloves roasted garlic

1 tsp. chopped fresh rosemary

1 Tbsp. unsalted butter, melted

SAUCE
1 cup veal stock

¼ cup Cinzano or other dry white vermouth

1 tsp. grainy Dijon mustard

1 tsp. unsalted butter

Braised Fillet of Halibut
with Asparagus and Wild Mushrooms

LEMON BUTTER
4 Tbsp. unsalted butter, room temperature

1 tsp. finely minced lemon zest

1 Tbsp. fresh lemon juice

VEGETABLES
20 stalks asparagus, trimmed

12 small new potatoes

4 tsp. vegetable oil

3 to 4 wild mushrooms, sliced

2 handfuls spinach, well dried

HALIBUT
2 Tbsp. unsalted butter

4 shallots, sliced

6 to 8 large mushrooms, sliced

1 cup Noilly Prat or other dry white vermouth

4 fillets halibut, each 5 oz.

¼ cup whipping cream, lightly whipped

IF YOU CANNOT FIND wild mushrooms, substitute a tasty cultivated variety such as shiitakes. The lemon butter can be made ahead and wrapped in plastic wrap; will keep refrigerated for up to 7 days, or in the freezer for up to 30 days. *Serves 4*

LEMON BUTTER: Place butter, lemon zest and juice in a bowl. Use a fork to mix until well combined. Season with salt and pepper. Cover with plastic wrap until needed.

VEGETABLES: Bring 2 saucepans of salted water to a boil on high heat. Add asparagus to 1 saucepan and potatoes to the other. Cook asparagus for 3 to 4 minutes, until just tender, then drain. Boil potatoes for 10 minutes, or until fork-tender, then drain. Keep asparagus and potatoes warm.

HALIBUT: Preheat the oven to 140°F.

Melt butter in a large ovenproof frying pan on medium heat. Sauté shallots and mushrooms for about 10 minutes, until soft. Stir in vermouth, turn up the heat to medium-high and cook for about 5 minutes, until the liquid is reduced to half. Add halibut. Coat each fillet with 2 tsp. of the lemon butter. Bring the sauce to a simmer, then cover the pan with a lid and cook for 1 to 2 minutes. Transfer the frying pan, covered, to the oven and cook for 5 minutes, until halibut is just cooked through. Transfer fish to a warm plate and save the pan juices.

FINISH VEGETABLES: Heat 2 tsp. of the oil in a frying pan on medium-high heat. Sauté mushrooms for 5 to 8 minutes, until tender and browned. Transfer to a bowl and keep warm.

Add the remaining oil to the frying pan. Sauté spinach for 3 to 4 minutes, until wilted. Drain, then keep warm.

FINISH HALIBUT: Strain the reserved pan juices through a fine-mesh sieve into a small saucepan on medium-high heat. Discard solids, including mushrooms and shallots. Cook for 5 minutes, until juices are reduced to ½ cup.

TO SERVE: Place a mound of spinach in the middle of each plate and top with a fillet of halibut. Spoon the sautéed wild mushrooms over the halibut. Arrange potatoes and asparagus on the side.

Stir cream into the pan juices, then season with salt and pepper. Froth with a hand-held blender or a whisk and pour over food on each plate.

WINE: Asparagus and wild mushrooms pair well with Sauvignon Blanc Private Reserve from Sumac Ridge.

Flakey Butter
Buns
$4.25/8

Tarte Bourdaloue

THIS PEAR AND ALMOND tart is a traditional French dish. For a truly beautiful and decadent dessert, serve it with crème anglaise, flavoured with Poire William, on the side. *Serves 8*

Preheat the oven to 325°F.

Place water, 1¾ cups of the sugar and vanilla in a saucepan on medium-high heat. Bring to a boil. Turn down the heat to low. Add pears and simmer for about 10 minutes, until soft but not mushy.

Combine butter, the remaining sugar and almonds in the bowl of an electric mixer. Add eggs, one at a time, beating slowing until well mixed. Fold in flour. Spoon this almond cream into a piping bag fitted with a plain tip. Fill the pie shell three quarters full with almond cream. Arrange pear halves, flat side down and pointed ends toward the middle, on top of the almond cream. Bake in the oven for 30 to 40 minutes, until almond cream is golden and puffed.

Trim off and discard any of the pie shell that is above the level of the pears.

Place apricot jam in a bowl and melt in a microwave oven on medium heat. Strain through a fine-mesh sieve and brush over warm tart to glaze the top.

TO SERVE: Cut the tart into 8 equal portions. Serve warm.

WINE: Gehringer Brothers' very sweet Minus 9 Ehrenfelser icewine can match this dish or follow it as a second dessert.

4 cups water

2¾ cups + 3 Tbsp. berry sugar

4 vanilla pods, slit lengthwise

4 Bosc or Bartlett pears, peeled, cored and halved lengthwise

1 cup unsalted butter, softened

1 cup ground almonds

3 eggs

⅓ cup all-purpose flour

1 prebaked pie shell, 10-inch diameter, 1½ inches deep

⅓ cup apricot jam

Cucumber and Winter Melon Salad

CHILI OIL

½ cup vegetable oil

1 tsp. paprika

1 tsp. cracked dried chilies

2 cloves garlic, crushed

SALAD

1 Tbsp. sambal oelek

⅓ cup mirin (page 13)

⅓ cup rice vinegar

1 lime, juice of

2 Tbsp. finely julienned
pickled ginger

1 tsp. salt

1 tsp. sugar

1 long English cucumber,
peeled, deseeded,
in sticks ½ × 2 inches

½ winter melon,
peeled, deseeded,
in sticks ½ × 2 inches

GARNISH

8 sui choy leaves

2 cups pea shoots

4 to 5 green onions, julienned

1 Tbsp. white sesame seeds

1 Tbsp. black sesame seeds

¼ cup julienned
crystallized ginger

FOR BEST RESULTS, marinate this salad overnight. The chili oil will keep in the refrigerator for up to 7 days. *Serves 4*

CHILI OIL: Heat oil in a frying pan on medium-high heat. Sauté paprika, chilies and garlic for about 5 minutes, until garlic browns and chilies sizzle. Strain through a fine-mesh sieve into a clean bowl and discard the solids. Let oil cool. If not using right away, cover and refrigerate.

SALAD: Combine sambal oelek, mirin, vinegar, lime juice, pickled ginger, salt and sugar in a bowl. Add cucumber and winter melon, then toss to coat. Cover and let marinate for at least 2 hours in the refrigerator.

TO SERVE: Line each salad bowl with 2 sui choy leaves. Place salad on top of the sui choy.

Heat chili oil in a saucepan on medium-high heat for about 30 seconds, until it begins to smoke, then pour some over each salad. Garnish with pea shoots, green onions, white and black sesame seeds and crystallized ginger.

WINE: The light crisp pineapple of Poplar Grove Pinot Gris complements the cucumber and winter melon.

Cucumber and Winter Melon Salad

Charred Beef Tenderloin with Zong Bao Triangles

RICE TRIANGLES

1 cup medium-grain white rice
(such as Calrose)

1 piece kombu, about
2 inches square, wiped lightly
with a dry cloth (page 13)

1 Tbsp. sugar

½ tsp. salt

2 Tbsp. rice vinegar

3 to 4 Tbsp. vegetable oil

BEEF

1 cup dried shiitake
mushrooms

1 tsp. salt

1 Tbsp. finely chopped
fresh garlic

1 Tbsp. finely chopped shallot

1 tsp. finely chopped fresh ginger

1 Tbsp. vegetable oil

12 to 14 oz. beef tenderloin,
trimmed of fat and sinew

DRIED SHIITAKE MUSHROOMS are sometimes called *fah koo.* Kecap manis is a sweetened soy sauce. Both are sold in Asian specialty stores.

As a general rule, do not refrigerate cooked rice or it will dry out. However, to save time, you can make the Zong Bao triangles ahead, except for the frying, and refrigerate them overnight. You can also rewarm the triangles in a 350°F oven for 5 minutes. For even faster preparation, serve steamed basmati or jasmine rice instead. *Serves 4*

RICE TRIANGLES: Wash rice under cold water until the water runs clear. Drain well. Place rice, 1¼ cups cold water and kombu in a heavy saucepan, cover with a lid and let soak for 30 minutes. Remove the lid and discard the kombu. Bring rice to a boil on medium-high heat, then turn down the heat to low. Cover with a lid and cook for about 15 minutes, until water is absorbed and rice is just tender. Remove from the heat and let rice sit, covered, for 15 minutes.

While the rice is cooking, combine sugar, salt and vinegar in a saucepan on low heat. Stir to dissolve sugar and salt.

Line a cookie sheet with parchment paper. Transfer the cooked rice to a large glass bowl. Drizzle the seasoned vinegar over the rice. Use a wooden spoon to gently stir rice to fluff it and coat it with the vinegar mixture. Spread rice evenly over the cookie sheet to a thickness of ½ inch and let cool to room temperature, then refrigerate for 1 to 2 hours.

BEEF: Roughly chop dried mushrooms, then grind them in a food processor or a coffee grinder. Combine the mushroom powder, salt, garlic, shallot, ginger and oil in a bowl. Mix the marinade well.

Cut beef tenderloin into 4 steaks, place on a plate and coat both sides with marinade. Cover with plastic wrap and refrigerate for 1 to 2 hours.

FINISH RICE TRIANGLES: Cut rice into six 4-inch squares. Cut each square in half diagonally to make triangles. Heat oil in a deep-sided heavy frying pan on medium heat until it begins to smoke. Carefully place 2 triangles at a time into the oil and fry for about 3 to 4 minutes per side, until golden brown. Drain on paper towels, then place on a cookie sheet and keep warm in the oven. Fry the remaining triangles and place each batch in the oven to keep warm.

FINISH BEEF: Preheat the barbecue or broiler to medium-high heat. Grill steaks for 3 to 4 minutes per side, until cooked to desired doneness. Let rest for 5 minutes, then carve into ¼-inch thick slices.

VEGETABLES: Heat oil in a heavy frying pan on medium-high heat. Sauté portobello and shiitake mushrooms for 5 minutes. Add cloud ear mushrooms and wine, then cook for 8 to 10 minutes, until the liquid is reduced a bit. Season with salt. Place spinach on top of warm mushrooms to wilt, then remove from heat.

SAUCES: Make one sauce by whisking together kecap manis, mirin and tamarind paste in a bowl. Make the other sauce in another bowl by whisking together hoisin sauce and vinegar.

TO SERVE: Place a warm rice triangle on each plate and top with 1 spoonful of the vegetable mixture and 1 slice of beef. Drizzle with each of the two sauces. Cover with a second rice triangle, vegetable mixture, beef and another drizzle of each of the two sauces. Top with a third triangle and repeat the layering.

WINE: Sweet soy and spice call for Jackson-Triggs Proprietors' Grand Reserve jammy Shiraz.

VEGETABLES

2 to 3 Tbsp. vegetable oil

3 large portobello mushroom caps, in ½-inch slices

8 shiitake mushroom caps, in ½-inch slices

2 cups dried cloud ear mushrooms, reconstituted with boiling water

4 Tbsp. dry white wine or chicken stock

1 lb. spinach leaves, stems removed

SAUCES

⅓ cup kecap manis

1 Tbsp. mirin (page 13)

1 Tbsp. tamarind paste

⅓ cup hoisin sauce

1 Tbsp. rice vinegar

Pallotte cac'e ove

(Cheese and Egg Balls)

1 cup milk

1 cup grated Parmigiano-
Reggiano cheese,
plus some for garnish

1 cup grated Pecorino cheese

6 eggs

2 cloves garlic, mashed

¼ tsp. freshly ground
black pepper

12 oz. day-old dried bread,
crusts removed

½ cup finely chopped
fresh parsley

3 Tbsp. extra-virgin olive oil

THIS SIMPLE DISH, which is similar to a light gnocchi, gets its name from a recipe typical of the Abruzzo region. *Cacio e uova,* as it is called there, is made during the hunting season. *Uova* is the Italian word for "eggs." *Serves 6 as an appetizer*

Combine milk, Parmigiano-Reggiano, Pecorino, eggs, garlic and black pepper in a bowl.

Place bread in a food processor and pulse until the bread has the consistency of coarse crumbs. Add bread to the egg mixture, then cover with plastic wrap and soak the bread overnight in the refrigerator. The mixture should resemble dough. Add parsley. Form into 1-inch balls.

Heat oil in a frying pan on medium-high heat. Sauté bread balls for about 5 to 6 minutes, until golden. Drain on paper towels. Season with salt, if necessary.

TO SERVE: Serve these on their own (or with a light tomato sauce), sprinkled with some grated Parmigiano-Reggiano.

WINE: Serve with an appetizer white wine such as crisp, refreshing CedarCreek Sauvignon Blanc Semillon with gooseberry, pear, melon and figs.

Chef Biographies

Numbers beside individual biographies refer to photos on title page spread (pages ii and iii).

MICHAEL ALLEMEIER *Mission Hill Family Estate Winery* South African–born Michael Allemeier began his career at age eleven, after baking his mother's birthday cake. Since then he has worked to critical and popular acclaim at Bishop's, Fairmont Chateau Whistler and Calgary's Teatro. Also a star of Food Network Canada's *Cook Like a Chef,* Allemeier can now be found scouring the farms and orchards of the Okanagan Valley, sourcing outstanding ingredients for his seasonally driven menus. Working closely with his repertoire of wines for Mission Hill's varied dining venues, he believes in using his food to "enhance, complement and occasionally contrast with a menu."

MURRAY BANCROFT *Restaurant Consultant and Food Stylist* When a younger Murray Bancroft caught a sea cucumber in the coastal waters off Vancouver, he was determined not to throw back the only catch of the day. He consulted the *Larousse Gastronomique,* and thus began his passion for food. After travelling and studying abroad, including two years in the south of France, Bancroft returned to Vancouver, where he has worked as a chef, corporate chef and food stylist. He has co-hosted *Barely Cooking,* a decidedly tongue-in-cheek cooking show that aired in four countries, and writes about food for *Vancouver* magazine and *Western Living.* He also authored the dining chapter for *Vancouver: The Unknown City.*

1 | KAREN BARNABY *The Fish House in Stanley Park* "Self-taught, on the job and by the seat of my pants," is how Karen Barnaby describes herself. Both an acclaimed cookbook author—*Pacific Passions* and *Screamingly Good Food*—and an exceptional chef, she also volunteers time for projects such as the *Many Hands* cookbook, written to support Vancouver's community kitchens. She takes her job seriously and is disappointed that some newcomers to the industry do not. But a self-deprecating sense of humour and "having it pointed out to me mid-career that I was a complete butt-head" have helped her succeed, make changes when necessary and keep her cooking fresh.

2 | SAM BENEDETTO *Temple Restaurant* Sam Benedetto understands that "You don't need to use exotic ingredients in order to achieve exotic results," and this kind of thinking has helped him place well up on *enRoute* magazine's Best New Restaurants list. A Sooke Harbour House prodigy, Benedetto is a member of the Island Chef's Collaborative, and emphasizes the importance of working and networking with farmers. He believes that British Columbia chefs have "harnessed the potential of our growing seasons and have renewed interest in small farming practices to the point of emerging as a top culinary destination."

3 | JEAN-YVES BENOIT *L'Emotion* Born in the aptly named Bouche-de-Rhone, France, Jean-Yves Benoit was sous-chef at a Michelin-starred restaurant by the age of twenty-two and soon had his own establishment in the Lubéron region. Recently arrived in Vancouver to raise a family, Benoit and his wife, Minna, have renovated an aging property in West Vancouver and opened it as a restaurant that has quickly caught critical and popular attention. Benoit has a passion "to serve the best possible seasonal produce and quality every day." Crediting his wife for running the dining room and keeping the books organized connects neatly with his motto: "To keep modest and humble."

JOHN BLAKELEY *Bistro Pastis* Born in Zimbabwe, trained in France and now serving up some of the city's best bistro cooking, John Blakeley got his start in Vancouver at the Four Seasons' Le Pavillion. He went on to work at some of Vancouver's finest restaurants including L'Orangerie, Café de Paris, Le Crocodile and Diva at the Met. In May 1999 he opened Bistro Pastis, an intimate neighbourhood bistro serving traditional French fare. A dedicated cyclist and triathlete, Blakeley's engaging manner and puckish smile continue to improve the lives of those he serves—especially when poised over his annual "Tour de France" tasting menus.

4 | JULIAN BOND *Dubrulle International Culinary Arts at the Arts Institute* With talent and grace, Julian Bond is leaving his mark on the culinary world. In 1999, he earned accolades from the *Globe and Mail* as Young Chef of the Millennium, then *Maclean's* voted him one of the top hundred Canadians under thirty, even though he is British. After apprenticing with the Fairmont chain, he became co-owner of Star Anise, then executive chef at the Le Soleil. He now directs culinary programs, teaching young chefs at Canada's largest and oldest private culinary school.

5 | BERNARD CASAVANT *Chef Bernard's Café* During his eight years as executive chef at the Fairmont Chateau Whistler (preceded by an impressively diverse professional background), Bernard Casavant set a trend in British Columbian culinary circles by celebrating local products and supporting local farmers and food purveyors. He has been a mentor to a number of young chefs and an inspiration to many of his contemporaries. Several years ago, he opened Chef Bernard's (and a successful catering firm), which is equally popular with locals and the tourists who congratulate themselves on finding it. Casavant represented Canada at the Bocuse d'Or world cuisine contest in 1991.

6 | CAROL CHOW *Hart House* Carol Chow was recruited by Umberto Menghi right after graduating from Dubrulle International Culinary Arts at the Arts Institute. She went on to chef at Bishop's, where she learned the value and importance of regional cuisine. For the past ten years, including a lengthy tour at the Beachside Café, she has been "promoting B.C. to a great extent, and with reason—we are utilizing local ingredients and working with our farmers, fishermen and other suppliers." Her passion for regional ingredients and her attitude toward cooking—"simplicity speaks for itself"—resonates in her dishes.

7 | ROBERT CLARK *C Restaurant* Of the eighty-two species of indigenous coastal seafood, Clark moves more onto the plate than any other chef on the coast. It might be challenging: smoked octopus "bacon" wrapped around an Alaskan king scallop. But equally, Clark is concerned about the sustainability of what he serves and how it's caught—halibut and salmon are often live-tanked. He believes British Columbia has become an emerging culinary destination due to "the hard work and dedication of a growing number of quality farmers, producers and suppliers."

8 | SEAN COUSINS *Raincity Grill* As much as his time in the kitchen counts, Sean Cousins' days off are equally important for searching out yet more local suppliers or foraging for indigenous ingredients himself. Hard-won skills have come via his mentor, C Restaurant chef Robert Clark, whose philosophy is "to discover and understand contemporary skills after working in many classical environments." Cousins' goal is to take Raincity Grill to using "99 per cent local foods," and to deliver those ingredients "as clean and as pure as possible."

9 | MICHAEL DEUTSCH *Fleuri Restaurant at the Sutton Place Hotel* In 2002, Michael Deutsch travelled to France and worked in six different restaurants over a period of two weeks. Now he promotes "daring and much-needed risks in flavour." He also believes in his staff and enjoys "the challenges of keeping staff motivated . . . . I enjoy listening to my team members present new ideas and ensuring that there is constant and creative positive energy in my kitchen." And Deutsch continually reinvests in his team: "My kitchen brigade has a wealth of ethnic diversity and all play an integral role in menu design and creation."

10 | ERNST DORFLER *The Five Sails Restaurant at the Pan Pacific Hotel* World traveller Ernst Dorfler has cooked in South Africa, Germany, Switzerland and his native Austria, but now calls Vancouver home. After apprenticing at the four-star Trattlerhof Hotel in Bad Kleinkirchenheim, he "also made several stops across Canada before becoming the executive chef at the five-diamond Pan Pacific Hotel in 1988. From 1981 to 1992, he competed extensively in local and international culinary com-petitions, earning more than thirty gold medals. His highlight came as a member of the Canadian team that earned Best Overall Team/Country honours at the 1992 International Culinary Olympics in Frankfurt.

11 | ANDREY DURBACH *Parkside* Barely thirty and already a veteran, Andrey Durbach is a local hero for his lusty flavours, deep reductions and smartly chosen wine card. His storied entrance into Vancouver's dining firmament began at Etoile and Lucy Mae Brown, followed by stints in Japan and England. Now he's chef and co-owner of the West End's prettiest room, complete with a soothing patio. It's a great fit. Although Durbach likes to challenge his customers to an increased "openness to new things," he believes that "good cooking is about doing simple, basic things incredibly well. Sound cooking techniques should always take precedence over trends."

12 | BRADFORD ELLIS *Quattro on Fourth* On Bradford Ellis's night off, you might actually find him dining at Quattro, studying the crowd and looking at the food through their eyes. A graduate of Vancouver Community College's Culinary Arts Program, he believes that "hard work and sacrifice equal success" for both him and his crew. Quattro has become a runaway hit on Vancouver's west side, full of neighbours and destination diners finding comfort in his relaxed menus of definitive antipasti, husky pastas and marinated hens. "Follow the lead of the best products," he says.

13 | ROB FEENIE *Lumière, Lumière Tasting Bar, Feenie's* Rob Feenie has become Canada's best-known chef (as anyone tuning into Food Network Canada can attest), yet he is quick to praise others, particularly Michel Jacob at Le Crocodile, who "taught me how important it was to be correctly trained, to excel at the basics before moving on to the creative side." From the significant accolades that Feenie and his restaurants have garnered—including being the first freestanding restaurant in Canada to receive the Relais Gourmands designation—it is clear that he has learned well. Feenie adds, "Simplicity is much more difficult to achieve than complicated cuisine . . . no gimmicks, no unnecessary presentations— a total focus on flavour."

14 | MANUEL FERREIRA *Le Gavroche* Manuel Ferreira was raised in a traditional Portuguese family that believes good food and wine, when accompanied by stimulating conversation, is the stuff of life. After moving to Canada, he held several positions at Le Gavroche before becoming its owner in 1974. A fire at the restaurant two years ago inspired several changes: fresh decoration, a wine bar and a new menu, which features French country flavours made light. The wine cellar at Le Gavroche is one of the deepest in the country—Ferreira is a member of the American Wine Society and was inducted into La Commanderie de Bordeaux in November 2003.

15 | DAVID FOOT *Aria at the Westin Grand* David Foot's résumé covers Vancouver's fine dining landscape, from an apprenticeship at the Prow Restaurant to classical training at the William Tell to working with the Canadian Culinary Team. Now executive chef at the Westin Grand Hotel, Foot still believes in keeping "an open mind to everything from hamburgers to truffles . . . we are only as good as the last plate that goes out of the kitchen." And Foot makes sure that his kitchen brigade of twelve at Aria lives up to his credo. He also oversees catering at the hotel, sometimes for more than sixteen hundred guests. His greatest challenge? "Meeting the many deadlines that are thrown at me."

16 | JULIO GONZALEZ-PERINI *Villa del Lupo* Buenos Aires–born chef and proprietor Julio Gonzalez-Perini is disciplined, a mandatory quality when orchestrating Villa del Lupo seven nights a week. He delegates much to his staff, but his mantra is "consistency, consistency and consistency." Since opening the restaurant in 1990, Gonzalez-Perini has sought to "treat our employees the same way we treat our clients and our food: with integrity and respect." Although he is concerned about the "lack of seriousness some people have towards a complex business," he believes that great cooking should be based in an essential simplicity.

17 | DENNIS GREEN *Bishop's* John Bishop would be the first to credit executive chef Dennis Green for his contribution to the success of Bishop's, where he started as sous-chef more than a decade ago. As well as co-authoring *Simply Bishop's* with his mentor, Green's recipes have been featured in *Gourmet* and *Canadian Living*. His success comes from his ability to listen and in his belief that everyone in the kitchen has something to add. His ingredient-driven, all-organic cooking continues to lead the way for the restaurant that invented Vancouver's culinary sense of place.

18 | ROLF GUNTER *Rim Rock Café & Oyster Bar*
A Whistler resident for twenty-six years, co-proprietor Rolf Gunter's culinary experience includes training at the four-star Park Hotel in Germany, hotel and restaurant management in Heidelberg and chef positions at several top hotels across Canada. As the creative force of the Rim Rock kitchen, he also stresses the importance of "knowing what my customers want— which might not always coincide with what I want to cook." And he's happy working a ten-hour day with his team, knowing there's nothing better to relieve the stress than "ripping it up on a snow or surf board."

19 | THOMAS HAAS *Diva at the Met/Senses Bakery*
Just two years ago, Thomas Haas won all four major categories at the U.S. National Pastry competition. For third-generation pastry man Haas, that was all in a day's work—or play, because he believes that success is "knowing what you are doing, loving what you are doing and believing in what you are doing." He left Vancouver to open Restaurant Daniel in New York City, but returned here with his wife, Lisa, to raise their family. Enthusiastic, energetic and deeply caring for his brigade, Haas now creates famous last courses for both Senses and the Metropolitan Hotel, and has launched a successful line of signature chocolates.

20 | DAVID HAWKSWORTH *West* David Hawksworth launched Ouest three years ago after a decade cooking in Europe beside such luminaries as Marco Pierre White and Bruno Loubet. Now known as West, the restaurant's name change signals a new comfort with the local ingredients and the emerging culinary landscape of his hometown. "What you get out of something is a direct measure of the amount of effort you are prepared to put in," he says. He applies this philosophy to the food he creates and the way he runs his restaurant, and it's paying off. In just his second year back, Hawksworth won *Vancouver* magazine's Restaurant of the Year Award.

21 | PETER HUYNH *Phnom Penh* Chef Peter Huynh's greatest challenge, and one he has succeeded at, was the jump from Japanese and Chinese cooking to, ironically, his native Vietnamese and Cambodian cuisine—not an easy task, given the many layers of flavours, techniques and ingredients. Now that he's firmly mastered the menu (and that the *New York Times* raved about the food at Phnom Penh), Huynh can concentrate on the daily operation of the restaurant, finding ways to "improve it, to constantly make it better."

22 | STUART IRVING *Wild Rice* Stuart Irving has learned that to "make enough money to pay the mortgage, win awards and good reviews, you must work harder than everyone else around you." Several years of martial arts training have also helped him to develop the discipline and focus necessary to control a busy kitchen. After making his mark in Vancouver at Bin 941 by creating innovative small plates, Irving jumped at the chance to open Wild Rice, a modern take on Chinese cooking, and with the bonus of exciting beverages. He has learned that "if you're not giving it your all every day, the cookie just crumbles."

23 | MICHEL JACOB *Le Crocodile* Twenty years on, Le Crocodile celebrates Alsace on the Pacific. Chef and propriétaire Michel Jacob's revelatory culinary moment was a meal at the legendary Au Crocodile, the three-macaron restaurant in his native Strasbourg. It was "unlike anything I had ever seen or tasted before," Jacob says, "and the fires were lit." Focussed, intense and with a supreme dislike for bland food, Jacob hopes that the home cook will strongly connect with these recipes, the better to find a common ground with each chef.

24 | SCOTT JAEGER *The Pear Tree* Not all of Vancouver's top restaurants are within its city limits. Take the Pear Tree in Burnaby, Scott Jaeger's fine dining restaurant that's a destination for those in the culinary know. "Compromise for no one" is Jaeger's motto, and his cooking continues to draw raves and an impressive array of awards, including *Vancouver* magazine's Best New Restaurant Award in 1998 and its Best of the 'Burbs Award virtually every year since. Jaeger believes that Vancouver is a culinary destination due to the "quality and attitude of the people in the industry, from growers to apprentices, servers and cooks."

25 | KRISHNA JAMAL *Rubina Tandoori, Rubina Grill* Chef Krishna Jamal is as natural and understated as her style of cooking. Completely self-taught, she believes that "there are no wrong ways of cooking food," adding only, "as long as everybody is on the same page on new projects." She salutes "the joy of being able to share my style of food with this city." That food is cleanly arced Indian, with flavours rampant then combining. Jamal is clearly a visionary, and her family's restaurant and smartly styled new express takeaway outlets add texture and warmth to the town.

26 | MARK JORUNDSON *Rocky Mountaineer Railtours* Cooking on a train is complicated by logistical, preparation and service challenges, and that's why Mark Jorundson's mantra when the kitchen gets too crazy is simply "Patience." The executive chef of *Rocky Mountaineer*'s Goldleaf Service, Jorundson and his team regularly serve 2,800 freshly cooked meals during the two-day journey through British Columbia and Alberta. He adds, "Recipes and meals don't always work out, but if you keep trying, you will eat perfection." He knows—Jorundson has represented Canada well at the International Culinary Olympics in Frankfurt.

27 | SCOTT KIDD *Dubrulle International Culinary Arts at the Arts Institute* Had Scott Kidd not decided to travel Europe after his third year of university, many deserving palates would have missed out. He abandoned his medical studies to train at the Cordon Bleu school in Sussex, England, then deconstructed New British cuisine in London under Anthony Worrall Thomson. In Vancouver, he promoted West Coast cuisine while working at Le Gavroche, Bishop's and the William Tell, and, along with other Top Table chefs, prepared a memorable meal at James Beard House in New York. Now back at school, he both teaches aspiring chefs at Dubrulle and is studying for a degree in agricultural food science.

28 | MICHAEL KNOWLSON *Bacchus Restaurant at the Wedgewood Hotel* "I spend more time with my sous-chef than with my wife," says English-born Michael Knowlson, who has recently been elevated to executive chef at the Wedgewood Hotel. Although he has travelled extensively, Knowlson credits his parents with setting him on the road to becoming a chef. Because of being surrounded by "incredible smells, tastes and ingredients," he confesses "the kitchen was the place I grew up in and found my passion." His skills are now being challenged by the complex food service requirements of a boutique hotel property, especially the legendary French menus at Bacchus.

29 | HIROSHI KUDO *Japone* Chef Hiroshi Kudo believes that "there is no perfect dish because everyone has different taste. We just enjoy trying to please each customer." Kudo learned his most important lessons from his father: hard work pays off, and believe in yourself—"do not trust someone else's opinion." Having said that, the most important part of his job right now is to "trust all of my employees." Ah, the Zen of life and cooking brought to the other side of the Pacific.

30 | LYNDA LAROUCHE *Seasons in the Park* With her restaurant's panoramic view of the mountains and downtown, Linda Larouche has one of the best offices in town. But it is also a busy room, with several private dining parties nightly and a steady tourist clientele most of the year. Although she loves her work, it can be stressful, especially "dealing with suppliers if something is not available, and making sure the kitchen is running efficiently." One important aspect of her job now is "making sure the staff understands and sees my vision." To avoid stress Larouche takes a walk in Queen Elizabeth Park before service, and yes, she stops to smell the roses.

31 | CHRISTOPHE LETARD *The Aerie* French-born Christophe Letard calls his last four years at the Aerie "a blast," citing his suppliers and his kitchen brigade as the main reasons. Collectively, he says, they are "the important parts that generate creativity, energy and flow." Letard works tirelessly to promote Vancouver Island as a fine food destination. He is a member of the Island Chef's Collaborative and has played a large part in shaping its culinary identity, believing that "the best is yet to come because of the abundance and potential of our rising talent."

32 | DON LETENDRE *Elixir at the Opus Hotel* Local boy Don Letendre went global, cooking Italian food in Japan for two years at Domani Cucina, where he picked up an invaluable lesson from his Japanese mentor: "To be a great chef you must believe in your hand—from how you handle food to the level of respect that you give your product." Letendre believes that cooking "starts with teaching, then finding the right product in the full potential of the season." About his kitchen brigade, Letendre says the secret is to "watch them grow and give them freedom without attitude."

33 | DAVID LONG *Terminal City Club* Executive chef David Long's earliest memories are of "sitting on the counter top in the kitchen while Mum baked." By age sixteen, he was an apprentice chef at the Shelbourne Hotel in Dublin, then by the late 1970s Northern Ireland's Chef of the Year. He's done Mum proud. These days, Long is "teaching, organizing, cooking, having fun" and relying on his kitchen team because "without them I am just a bunch of ideas." Running a large operation, Long has also learned that "chefs should be in the kitchen with their brigade and not stuck in meetings."

34 | GORD MARTIN *Bin 941/942* If Vancouver is known for its tasting menus, it's in no small part because of Gord Martin, chef-owner of the two Bins. Homegrown but widely travelled—with cooking stints in Italy, Morocco, Turkey and Mexico, Martin learned the important ingredients of love, passion and dedication. He credits the province's hard-working farmers, and their growing array of ingredients, for British Columbia's growth as a culinary destination. Martin himself is constantly sourcing sustainable and responsibly harvested meats, fish and produce while keeping costs in line to produce an affordable menu of playful, award-winning tapas known for their big, bold flavours.

35 | STEPHANE MEYER *Piccolo Mondo Ristorante* Even though executive chef Stephane Meyer has been a two-star Michelin chef in his native France, he knows the importance of humility: "You never know everything; even if you are a head chef, you are always learning, maybe new products, maybe different techniques." For his success, Meyer credits his mother: "She can cook dinner for ten in half an hour," and chef Didier Oudill, who "cooks to fine dining levels with cheap ingredients." Now he is passing on his own knowledge to fellow cooks and customers, and "sharing my passion, my pleasure of culinary art and the happiness that I have while cooking."

36 | MORENO MIOTTO *Bis Moreno* From Prince George to Vancouver, with stops in Toronto and Beverly Hills, Moreno Miotto has worked hard to realize his dream. Bis Moreno—voted Best New Restaurant in 2004 by *Vancouver* magazine—is the culmination of many years of learning. He apprenticed with Giorgio Baldi of Forte di Marni in California, followed by stints in such celebrated dining rooms as Chicco Ristorante and Il Ristorante di Giorgio Baldi. With his wife, Cinzia, he then opened Da Moreno in Prince George, where he worked for over a decade honing his skills. Now based in Vancouver, Miotto is a passionate perfectionist who hand picks all produce, meats and fish and makes his own homemade pasta daily.

37 | FRANK PABST *Blue Water Café and Raw Bar*
With a pedigree that includes an apprenticeship with Christof Lang at La Bécasse (Aachen), tours with Dominique LeStanc at Hotel Negresco (Nice), Serge Philippin at Restaurant de Bacon (Cap d'Antibes) and Daniel Ettlinger at Le Diamant Rose (Nice), Frank Pabst comes by his award-winning cooking skills honestly. He insists that his "ingredients are shown the respect they deserve; be it sustainable fish, line-caught by hard working fishermen in our regional waters, or heirloom vegetables that have been pampered on a field by a caring grower." He insists on the same respect for the people he works with. The results, as diners at Blue Water Café know, are superlative.

38 | ROBERT PARROTT *Gusto di Quattro* Robert Parrott has worked with the Corsi family, owners of Quattro restaurants, for as long as he can remember, opening all three restaurants. He is proof that you don't need to be Italian to cook real Italian food, it's really about "uncomplicated food with an integrity of flavours, integrating the best and freshest products available." On a recent trip to Italy, he studied how Italians take the proper time to eat, with "everything made to order and nothing rushed." Quality products and flavours are paramount, but so are "bringing new ideas to the staff, or bringing new ideas out of them."

39 | PINO POSTERARO *Cioppino's Mediterranean Grill, Cioppino's Enoteca* "The customer is always right, at least when he is not wrong," says Pino Posteraro. His customers must agree, because his take on pan-Mediterranean flavours is received by packed houses throughout the week. Cioppino's three private dining rooms and two bars are also popular, as much for their frequent industry accolades as for their warm bonhomie and professional staff. Posteraro is quick to point out that his kitchen brigade, floor staff and suppliers all contribute to the success of the restaurant, but the person he most looks up to, both as his teacher and culinary hero, is, quite simply, "my mother."

40 | ROMY PRASAD *Cin Cin Ristorante* Romy Prasad's résumé is studded with Michelin stars from France, Italy and Spain—a world away from Guyana, where he remembers his mother grinding spices by hand and pre-paring family meals on a wood-fired stove. It isn't just coincidence that he now creates dishes in Cin Cin's signature wood-fired oven. While working his way through university, Prasad attended Ontario's Stratford Chefs School and later enrolled in the Ritz Escoffier Cooking School in Paris. His cooking style reflects his classic European training blended with coastal flavours, amply displayed at his frequent forays to James Beard House in Manhattan.

41 | ALESSANDRA QUAGLIA *Provence Mediter-*
ranean Grill, Provence Marinaside

In between caring for two small children, chef-owner Alessandra Quaglia part- nered with husband Jean-Francis to open Provence Mediterranean Grill, then Provence Marinaside just a few years later. Although the restaurant is a challenge, she also focusses on her children. She believes in "doing what you know," which comes naturally to her, coming from a food- obsessed Danish family. She admonishes us to "eat well every day."

42 | JEAN-FRANCIS QUAGLIA *Provence Mediter-*
ranean Grill, Provence Marinaside

Marseille-born chef-proprietor Jean-Francis Quaglia readily credits his mother for his success, from her recipes to working in her restaurant. At eight, Jean-Francis made *tarte au citron* from her recipe, and after his apprenticeship, returned to his mother's restaurant as sous-chef. Meeting Ales- sandra, a Canadian, was a turning point— they married, moved to Vancouver and soon opened Provence. Although running a restaurant is a daily challenge, "dealing with the demands of staff, customers, equipment malfunctions, banking and whatever," Jean-Francis looks at the big pic- ture, of British Columbia as a "community of great chefs dedicated to food."

43 | MONTRI RATANARAJ *Montri's Thai Restaurant*

For consistently great Thai food, locals flock to Montri's. Born in Thailand, Ratanaraj himself presides over the kitchen and the consistently packed dining room, extending a warm welcome to his regulars. Educated in the culinary arts around the world, including an apprenticeship at Copenhagen's Royal Hotel and a stint cook- ing on cruise ships, he credits most of his learning to the chef of the Royal Family of Thailand, Mrs. Terb Xoomsai. To this day, he strives for consistency of flavour and attention to quality. "We are what we eat," he says, insisting that great food depends on fresh ingredients.

44 | DANA REINHARDT *Cru* With a résumé that includes the River Café in London, and Lumière and Raincity Grill in Vancouver, Dana Reinhardt was eager to launch Cru— her own kitchen. It's a challenge as chef and owner: "Not only do I have to concern myself with running a busy kitchen, I also have to be involved in all the decisions of running the restaurant." Husband and som- melier Mark Taylor and service director Christine Funnell share the load. The result is clean flavours on small plates, paired with an innovative wine list that won Taylor the Sommelier of the Year Award at the Vancouver Playhouse International Wine Festival.

45 | LALIT SHARMA *Maurya* "Stay cool and smile," says Lalit Sharma, "especially when it gets hot in the kitchen." Maurya is Vancouver's most beautiful Indian room; under soaring ceilings, a deep wine list is neatly matched to the spice and brimstone of Sharma's menu. Savour the Pacific halibut and local lamb lit from behind with traditional spicing. Sharma's philosophy: "Cook simple food that can be made and enjoyed by everyone."

ANDREW SPRINGETT *Pointe Restaurant at the Wickaninnish Inn* Canada's 2003 Bocuse d'Or competitor in Lyons, Andrew Springett earned his urban reputation at Diva at the Met, where the husky flavours of his cuisine drew critical praise and a popular following. Now executive chef at The Pointe Restaurant at Tofino's Wickaninnish Inn, he cooks in a distinctly coastal dialect that includes such ingredients as Pacific halibut, Skeena sockeye, Clayoquot oysters, Dungeness crab and smoked cod. It's only fitting, then, that these foods are served in the Pointe's oceanfront dining room, which overlooks Chesterman Beach and one of the most dramatic seascapes in Canada.

46 | GEORGE SZASZ *Paprika Bistro* In the beginning, there were the Hungarian delicatessens the Szasz family owned on Robson Street and South Granville. Under the watchful eyes of parents and grandparents, George Szasz learned his craft well. Today, he marries light and sometimes feisty Hungarian influences with coastal ingredients. Szasz and wife, Linda Mae, who worked at Bishop's for its first seven years, champion the philosophy of locality and sustainability, hoping that chefs will increasingly "look to their backyards for inspiration and support the farming community around us."

47 | HIDEKAZU TOJO *Tojo's* Since coming to Vancouver in the early 1970s from Onoya, where he learned the traditional basics of Japanese cookery (and memorized some two thousand recipes), Tojo-san has helped shape the city's culinary destiny. Often called the Elvis of sushi, this master transforms the freshest product of the ocean into intricate and innovative plates. His rigorous apprenticeship comprised sixteen-hour days but taught him that hard work and honesty would deliver his dreams. Today, Tojo-san is "training a new generation of chefs to follow in my footsteps, to step out of the traditional cooking methods and be creative." Follow Tojo's rule to find your dreams: "tastes good . . . looks good . . . good for you."

48 | TAKAHIRO TOYOSHIGE *Hapa Izakaya*

"Shige" Toyoshige places his customers first: "They help me improve my food, service and myself . . . . I always pay attention to how my customers react when they taste my dishes." Taste them they do: Hapa captured Vancouver's imagination as it rode the tsunami of the izakaya boom. Although it's still challenging to find certain Japanese ingredients, and usually more expensive, Toyoshige rises to the challenge "to cook the best with the ingredients at hand." After cooking for eight years in Tokyo, he would like "to make Japanese comfort food more popular in Canada," and is succeeding wildly: Hapa captured *Vancouver* magazine's special Editors' Choice honour in 2004.

49 | JEREMIE TROTTIER *Quattro at Whistler*

Key to Jeremie Trottier's career was his time working with a diverse group of cooks at the Hotel Vancouver, "because it allowed me to see several different styles of cooking, which I could then develop into my own." A summer trip to Italy with the Quattro team "made me even more passionate about our style of cooking. The best cooks we met never use freezers, they shop every day. It reminded me why it's so important to maintain that sort of ongoing connection with our own suppliers and food purveyors."

EDWARD TUSON *Sooke Harbour House*

After stints in the front trench at Vancouver's Wedgewood Hotel and Cin Cin, self-described culinary foot soldier Edward Tuson has cooked at Sooke Harbour House for the past thirteen years (with a few gaps in between). Tuson and his mentor, proprietor Sinclair Philip, have made their mark using the regional, seasonal, organic and wild foods of southern Vancouver Island, including spear-gunned fish, seaweed garnitures, wild and cultivated greens and herbs from Sooke's summer gardens. Their many apprentices have learned well. Now fanned out across the province, they too extol the virtues of what's closest at hand.

50 | VIKRAM VIJ *Vij's, Rangoli* As loyal customers will attest, Vancouver is a better place since Vikram Vij opened his namesake restaurant. It's a place culinary tourists want to cross off their lists, as is Rangoli, his next-door, all-day room. Thanks to stints at Bishop's and Raincity Grill, along with training in Europe, Vij has brought India to his new home in clean, unfettered flavours. Now, carefully ramped eastern tastes merge easily with regional foods, wines and microbrews. Vij maintains that "hard work, honesty, integrity and a love for what you do" spur him on. Lessons well learned: in 1999, Vij showcased at James Beard House in New York.

51 | GREGORY WALSH *Northlands Bar and Grill* The tone of Gregory Walsh's day is set in the first five minutes. And because he has "chosen a profession where I could be truly happy," the day is often to his liking. And to others: in the early 1990s, he became the opening chef at Raincity Grill and had Bryan Miller of the *New York Times* sit down and take notice, helping to establish the idea of Vancouver as a culinary destination. He has since received many awards for his cuisine. Humility, though, is his key to success: "Every quality a good chef must have: patience, presence and over the top confidence, all start with being humble."

52 | JAMES WALT *Araxi* James Walt honed his skills in classic French techniques at Sooke Harbour House, where he also learned extensively about fresh, local and organic products. Now, following several years at Bluewater Grill, James has returned to Whistler's Araxi—conveniently located near the farms of the Pemberton Valley that supply his restaurant with organic ingredients. He has been invited to cook at the James Beard House in New York City twice, and in 2000 the *Globe and Mail* named Walt one of the top 133 young Canadians shaping the nation, an honour bestowed on just five chefs across Canada.

53 | PETER ZAMBRI *Zambri's* There are three things Peter Zambri thanks for being where he is today: Moving to the west coast and working at Sooke Harbour House (kitchen and garden) when he was twenty-one years old, cooking in Italy and, finally, opening his own restaurant, Zambri's, in Victoria. As a member of the Island Chef's Collaborative and the Slow Food Organization, Zambri has direct contact with the people who grow the food he serves, and he believes "in fundamentally being true to the produce I am using." Uncomplicated yet passionate, Zambri advocates "spontaneity, determination and hard work."